Walt Disney World Dining Guide 2018

Andrea McGann Keech

Theme Park Press
The Happiest Books on Earth
www.ThemeParkPress.com

Editor: Bob McLain

Layout: Artisanal Text

ISBN 978-1-68390-067-2

Printed in the United States of America

Theme Park Press | www.ThemeParkPress.com

Address queries to bob@themeparkpress.com

For Katherine, Drew, and Will,
the sweetest trio

Contents

Introduction

To those who haven't yet read the Walt Disney World Dining Guide, *welcome. To those who've read an earlier edition, welcome back. In this latest addition, any new full service, casual, or quick service restaurants, as well as new carts and kiosks, will be reviewed; price and menu changes will be updated; and alterations to the Disney Dining Plan will be noted (for example, this is the first year alcoholic beverages and specialty drinks have been included as part of the dining plans). Pull up a seat, dig in, and don't forget to bring your appetite...*

Why in the Walt Disney World would you need to spend any of your valuable leisure time preparing six months (or more!) ahead of your vacation for exactly where, when, and what you plan to eat on your much-anticipated visit to the Most Magical Place on Earth? The fact that you'd even ask means you desperately need help—and fast! Without doing your homework many months before the first day of your trip, you'll miss out on some of the best experiences that can make a vacation at Walt Disney World so memorable.

If you have never visited Walt Disney World, or if it's been awhile since your last visit, you'll be surprised to discover how important it is these days to make Advance Dining Reservations. That's right, the phrase is capitalized and even has its own acronym: ADRs. Securing ADRs has become almost an art form. People across the country, and indeed the world, have their eager fingers poised above their keyboards ready to hit the "submit" button at the stroke of 6:00 a.m. Orlando time on the first day they are allowed to book those critical reservations. Don't be left out! This guide will ensure that *you* have the best chance to dine when and wherever you want.

Sampling entirely new flavors and cuisines, participating in one-of-a-kind themed dining experiences, and enjoying some of those unique Disney snacks only available at Walt Disney

World will add significantly to how much you and your family enjoy yourselves. It's surprising how much a character meal, dinner show, or a memorable dinner will add to the pleasure and enjoyment of your vacation.

Some dining guides jump back and forth like a pinball between the four theme parks (Magic Kingdom, Epcot, Animal Kingdom, Disney's Hollywood Studios), the Disney resort hotels, the BoardWalk, and Disney Springs. You're left spinning and overwhelmed. These guides are often divided into sections like "best kids meals" or "great snacks." You need to flip back and forth a thousand times comparing offerings among the various venues. As far as I'm concerned, that's not the easiest nor most useful way to get a good sense of where you'll want to eat on any given day of your vacation. As a Disneyland Tour Guide and VIP Hostess throughout college, I learned the importance of organizing any visit one area at a time. You'll be in *one* place at a time, not twenty, and that's exactly how this simple, informative guide is organized.

I won't often tell you what I like to eat because maybe, *probably*, you and I differ on our preferences. When a member of the wait staff says, "I'd suggest the scallops tonight—they're excellent," that doesn't help me because scallops are never my choice. Likewise, when a reviewer advises trying the fresh sashimi (raw fish) at Morimoto Asia, count me out. Honestly, I don't care what someone *else* likes; I want to know what a particular place has on its menu that *I* might like. A guide that gives you just one or two ideas from a menu, usually what the writer ate, simply isn't enough information to inform my decision.

While I won't list entire menus (you can see those online easily), I *will* tell you the types of foods, preparation styles, and special experiences you can expect at any given place. Food critics who detail just one meal at a restaurant miss the other fifty things I'd be willing to try before I'd ever choose the charred octopus or goat cheese ravioli. Therefore, I'll give you a very good idea of what you'll find at the many Walt Disney World places to dine. You decide which places have menu selections that are likely to please most members of *your* party.

Not only that, I've found some guides to be so extensive that unless you're *only* going to Disney World to eat, and you're not, they're too unwieldy to navigate and contain more information than you could use in two lifetimes. There's a limit to how many hundreds of pages you can wade through and how many hundreds of hours you're prepared to spend searching for relevant bits and pieces of information online. How much time are you willing to devote to sifting through the scattered entries of individual restaurants and evaluating the confusing array of websites?

It would take months to uncover for yourself all of the information I've put right here at your fingertips. I'd like to make your search for great food *easy*. It simply shouldn't require you to spend days, weeks, or months figuring out your vacation meals. Those of us who live in the real world are too busy with work and family to devote that kind of time to meal planning!

Whether your trip is an adults-only romantic getaway or a kid-friendly romp with an emphasis on the toddlers, tadpoles, tweens, or teens in the family, you *will* need to do some background research and make those key dining reservations six months in advance. Yes, you heard that last bit right: *six months* ahead of time. A full 180 days (and make that 180+10—see chapter 16, Twelve Tremendous Tips) before your vacation starts, you need to have your fingers poised above the screen on your iPhone, iPad, or computer. Be ready to go the second you are allowed to do so because every other savvy guest you'll be rubbing shoulders with during your upcoming vacation will be doing the exact same thing *and* doing it at the exact same moment.

Planning matters (more than you ever thought possible) when it comes to dining at Disney World, but it *can* be done with a reasonable effort. That's where this guide will help you. It will group the many choices into manageable sections you can skim quickly. It will highlight the best places to dine that will satisfy all members of your party.

You are on vacation to enjoy the attractions and the ambience, true, but without some sustenance, it's going to be a very rocky—and hungry—road, my friends. If you've ever been desperate to find a decent place to eat while starving children, famished teenagers, or peckish grandparents are complaining loudly in your ear and your own stomach is rumbling uncomfortably, you'll appreciate how much knowing *where* you are going, *when* you need to arrive there, and *what* you can expect to eat at those three meals a day can make the difference between unfortunate family feuds and happy tummies that will allow your group to continue on its merry way.

Look around at those families who *didn't* plan ahead like you to appreciate the value of having a workable meal-time itinerary. Those families aren't difficult to find. They're the ones with the tears, howls, and loud harrumphs. Luckily, that won't be you and your family.

Whether it's sitting down to Mickey waffles, bacon, and scrambled eggs with the kids at the Polynesian's 'Ohana character breakfast, complete with a rollicking meet-and-greet session with Lilo, Stitch, Mickey, and Pluto, or toasting your sweetheart with vintage champagne at the Grand Floridian's ultra-luxurious Victoria and Albert's while savoring the 10-course chef's tasting menu, careful planning ahead for your dining pleasure is absolutely key. Without some preparation, memorable meals at the best places in the resort with those you love best simply won't happen.

Don't get me wrong. There will be plenty of time during your visit for spontaneity, for grabbing something delicious on-the-go and savoring it as you head for the next attraction or shop for souvenirs. As long as you think ahead and make a plan, however, you won't miss out on some of the best dining options at Walt Disney World.

As Napoleon Bonaparte observed, "An army marches on its stomach." Well, so does a vacationer, and you have a lot of marching ahead of you. Now, dig in and let's get started!

Digesting the Disney Dining Plan

Originally, the Disney Dining Plan was offered as part of a holiday package at Walt Disney World. It proved to be so popular that it became a regular offering. At first, guests were delighted with the great value they received for the affordable price. Over the years, that value has eroded. Costs for the dining plans have risen to the point where you must be very sure you will take full advantage of your plan for it to make fiscal sense.

Before beginning an in-depth consideration of the merits of the Disney Dining Plan, there is something you should keep in mind: Disney is very definitely a for-profit corporation and doesn't make business decisions that will cause the company to lose money. The Disney Dining Plan has its pluses and minuses, but it is not intended to lose money for the organization. That said, in the first part of this guide we will consider the merits of the various Disney dining plans based on your specific needs and preferences.

Some visitors purchase these dining plans year after and year and are satisfied they are getting good value and convenience for the cost, while others count up hundreds of dollars they've wasted by purchasing dining plans for the family and say "never again." You'll need to carefully evaluate the type of consumer you are in order to determine whether or not the Disney Dining Plan makes good sense for you.

If you can say "yes" to the following, you *might* be a candidate for the Disney Dining Plan:

- I like the convenience of prepaying for things, even if it actually costs me a bit more in the long run.

- My vacations are run on a set schedule. I book FastPass+ six months in advance and don't mind deciding on what to eat, when, and where six month ahead.

- I like taking a break from all the action in the parks and sitting down to enjoy a leisurely, full-service meal with the family at least once each day.

- I'm something of a gourmet who enjoys trying lots of unique, exotic dishes and cuisines I wouldn't normally get to taste at home.

- I'll often choose the most expensive item on the menu and rarely skip dessert.

- I'm fine with learning and adhering to a complex set of rules, restrictions, and new vocabulary (table-service credits, ADRs, snack credits, etc.).

Disney's dining plans are *only* available to guests staying in one of the many Disney hotels and who book a Magic Your Way vacation package. I highly recommend that you *do* stay in Disney accommodations. That decision will save you a tremendous amount of time, and there are rooms available at many price levels, from deluxe suites to budget-friendly rooms to campsites. The expansive resort encompasses over 27,000 acres, and staying off-property adds significantly to your travel times to and from the resort every day.

If you decide to stay in *two* different Disney hotels during your stay at Walt Disney World, and this can be a great way to experience the best of what each hotel has to offer, then you *must* purchase *two* separate Disney dining plans. This would be a chance for you to try one of the dining plans for part of your vacation while you stay at one hotel and then eat on your own *without* a dining plan during the second part of the vacation at a second hotel. See which way you like best.

Just as with booking restaurant reservations, you should book your rooms at least *six months* in advance of your arrival. (If you speak directly with a cast member, you can sometimes book as far as 499 days in advance!) As soon as you know when you're coming, book your hotel room(s)! Some luxury villas are part of the Disney Vacation Club and have extremely limited availability. First come, first served means *you* need to be first!

Staying at a Disney hotel grants you these important *free* benefits:

- Travel to and from the Orlando Airport by a convenient motor coach called Disney's Magical Express.

- Skip the baggage claim after your flight. Luggage from your airline will be delivered directly to your resort hotel room.

- Get the incredibly helpful MagicBand for every member of your party. More on this handy little gadget later. You'll wonder how you ever got along without it.

- Schedule FastPass+ to popular attractions 60 days ahead of time (that's 30 days before people who aren't staying on Disney property can schedule them).

- Transportation by motor coach, monorail, or boat will be available at no charge between parks, to all resort hotels, and to Disney Springs and Disney's BoardWalk, including free parking if you've rented a car.

- A brand-new Skyliner transportation system is currently under construction that will soon link Disney's Pop Century, Art of Animation, and Caribbean Beach resorts with Hollywood Studios and Epcot.

- Minnie Vans provided through Lyft are being piloted for guests staying at Disney's Yacht Club, Beach Club and BoardWalk Inn. For $20, the red-and-white polka-dotted vans take you exactly when and where you want to go at Walt Disney World. No tipping is necessary or expected. If successful, the service is sure to be expanded to include other resort hotels.

- In-room free WiFi, which is also available in some restaurants and other public resort areas.

- Extra Magic Hours, hours either before opening or after closing times at the theme parks when only guests staying at Disney accommodations (and a few select others) will be able to come earlier or stay later than other guests in order to enjoy less crowded conditions. Not every park will have Extra Magic Hours every day.

As someone who has vacationed at Walt Disney World many times and stayed both on site and off, I strongly recommend staying in a Disney resort hotel. Not only will you receive the benefits listed above, you'll be right in the middle of the action at all times. Lengthy drives through former orange groves and Florida backcountry now bristling with tourist traps, hotels, and apartment complexes at the beginning and end of each day take up far too much of your limited time and energy, and can even kill the Disney vibe you woke up with. Unless you're staying with family or friends in the area, it makes a lot more sense to stay in one of the resort hotels.

Magic Your Way

There are currently some 25 Disney resort hotels, 4 major theme parks, Disney Springs, and the BoardWalk—that adds up to 150+ places to eat! When you book a Magic Your Way vacation package, you can reserve either a room and ticket package *or* a room, ticket, and dining package. That's when you need to decide if one of the Disney dining plans is right for your needs. You buy it at the same time as you book the Magic Your Way reservations. It *might* be possible for you to add the Disney Dining Plan at a later time to your pre-existing reservation, and sometimes you may be allowed to do so, but you would need to call and confirm whether that change is possible. Don't count on it. Any addition of the Disney Dining Plan must usually be done a minimum of 48 hours in advance of your arrival. Cases are considered on an individual basis. The time you book your reservation is also the time to make the staff aware of any special dietary restrictions you may have or to make any special food requests known.

Either download the My Disney Experience app free from the App Store online or call (407) 939-5277 or (407) WDW-MAGIC to make your hotel reservation. You'll find a large amount of useful information at disneyworld.disney. go.com, too. Disney resort hotels fall into five different price brackets: deluxe villas, deluxe resorts, moderate resorts, value resorts, and campsites. Check out Disney's online descriptions for a complete comparison of what each one has to offer. Prices for lodgings change frequently and without notice and will also vary by season.

Walt Disney World Resort Hotels

All of the hotels on Disney property offer dining options, some of them superlative like Victoria and Albert's, which has earned the rare Five Diamond AAA Award yearly since 2000, and others merely so-so. They are classified as fine/signature dining (the best of the best), unique/themed dining (part of what makes each venue special, including character buffets), casual (table service but relatively inexpensive), food courts (for your grab-and-go needs), lounges (some of them sumptuous, others casual), dining events (check with your hotel when you book your rooms for any special offerings available during your stay), and finally in-room dining (expensive room service, but sometimes it's just exactly what you need).

Deluxe Villas

Expect to pay a premium for this level of luxury. Prices *start* at $318 and rise swiftly and quite steeply from there, depending on the time of year, size of suite, view, and particular amenities available. You can spend around $1,000 a night or more for a deluxe villa including taxes and fees. Each of these deluxe hotels is special in a different way, and you may already have an idea of where you'd like to stay, but all villas generally offer spacious suites with well-stocked kitchens, laundry facilities in the unit, and multi-bedroom options for larger groups.

Deluxe Resorts

The deluxe hotels are located in the same hotel complexes as the villas, but prices for rooms begin at $307 per night, depending on the season. You won't have some of the amenities available at the villas (don't look for complete kitchens or laundry facilities), but the rooms will still be nicely appointed with many extras. All of the deluxe hotels offer in-room dining you can purchase using meal credits from the dining plan.

Moderate Resorts

Rooms in the moderate hotels are an excellent value with rates from $166 per night, depending on the season. You'll still get the Disney touches you want, with plenty of fun, creative themes carried throughout the hotel.

Value Resorts

Families on a tighter budget will appreciate the ability to stay on Disney property without breaking the bank on lodgings. Value rooms are priced from a wallet-friendly $97 per night to start, depending on the season. Don't look for pricy extras, but you can count on the fact that anything on the resort grounds will be impeccably maintained and clean. Staff will, with rare exceptions, be helpful and friendly. Best of all, you'll still qualify for the many free benefits listed at the beginning of this chapter. While you can't order in-room delivery service at a value resort, you can still have a pizza meal with beverage and dessert brought right to your room by using two dining plan credits.

Campsites

With prices for a campsite starting as low as $53 per night, Disney's 700-acre Fort Wilderness Resort offers one more level of flexibility for families looking to save money while still enjoying a wonderful Walt Disney World vacation. Campsites accommodate up to 10 people, are pet-friendly, and provide water, electrical hook-ups, and cable TV. If you decide to rent a cabin, from $381.38 and up, you can even advance-order an entire pantry full of grocery items that will be waiting for you when you arrive. There are two pools with waterslides, movies under the stars, an exercise trail, horseback and pony rides, bike and watercraft rentals, Chip 'n Dale's Campfire and Sing-a-long, a white sand beach, and a playground for the children.

What the Disney Dining Plan Does and Doesn't Do for You

You no longer have to worry about budgeting for meals while you're on vacation. It's all been taken care of. The plan is essentially a voucher system. You pay for what you will eat in advance and receive credits to spend every day at any of the participating places to eat in the parks—and there are many of them!

Credits are the currency you have available to spend on your meals and snacks every day. Your dining plan credits will be encoded onto your MagicBand and scanned when you wish to purchase food. All credits are not created equal. Some credits buy a table-service meal, some a quick-service meal, and some a snack. Some meals are considered two-credit meals (those at very elegant dining venues, Cinderella's Royal Table with the princesses in the castle, and one of the three dinner shows). Sometimes, you might decide to select items from a separate *prix fixe* menu offered at certain locations. That choice requires paying an extra charge in addition to redeeming meal credits. In recent years, many new dining establishments have joined the Disney Dining Plan including the popular Le Cellier Steakhouse in the Canada Pavilion of Epcot. The list of restaurants is fluid. It takes some time to work out contracts at the start of every new year, especially with non-Disney-owned dining establishments. Some may elect to join, while others may decide to drop out.

Sounds difficult keeping up with all those credits you use every day, doesn't it? Don't worry, because at the end of every meal, your remaining credit total will be clearly listed on your check. You can also ask your hotel's concierge to find out where you stand regarding credits spent and credits still available. You are free to spend any unused credits up until 11:59 p.m. on the day you check out of your resort hotel.

There is no charge on the Disney dining plans for children under three. Little ones are free to eat off your plate (literally), or you may want to order something else just for them, but you'll need to pay out-of-pocket for that. At a buffet where you will be serving yourself, you are allowed to get your children under three their *own* plate plus a beverage at no cost; this isn't true at quick-service or table-service meals. Children are only considered "children" up to age nine, and children on the dining plan are *only* able to order from the children's menu where one is available, not the adult menu. After they turn ten, they're considered adults and must pay as such and are supposed to order from the adult menu. What happens if your ten or eleven or twelve year old doesn't *like* anything on the adult menu? Special requests like that are often accommodated by giving the older child a larger portion of something from the children's menu. The over-nine-year-old, in that case, would still be charged a full credit for the meal.

Some things aren't included with *any* of the Disney dining plans:

- Multi-serving items intended for more than one person
- Things that come in a souvenir container
- Food and beverages sold at a recreation rental counter
- Things that are considered merchandise (bottle toppers, bottle straps, etc.)
- Certain dining events with special menus available at table-service restaurants

Bear in mind that gratuities are no longer included (with a very few exceptions, like Cinderella's Royal Table), so you are expected to tip the wait staff in addition to what you have already paid for the plan. With groups of six or more, 18% will be added *automatically* to your bill, even if one of those six guests is a six-month-old baby who hasn't eaten a thing.

One thing you *won't* be charged separately for is tax: it's included with the cost of the dining plan.

Tables in Wonderland

About one hundred restaurants at Walt Disney World participate in Tables in Wonderland, a program offering discounted meals for frequent guests. Members save 20% on their dining bills for up to ten people in the party. An 18% gratuity is added to your bill. One big benefit is that the membership comes with free valet parking provided you only come to dine. There are blocked-out dates throughout the year.

Tables in Wonderland is limited to Florida residents, DVC members, and Walt Disney World annual passholders. If you're one of those, and the program seems like a good value because you dine at Disney World often, you can buy an annual membership at the Guest Relations office in any of the four theme parks or at Disney Springs. Once you have your membership card, make sure you don't lose it: there is a $50 replacement charge.

Annual membership costs $175 for Florida residents, and $150 for DVC members and annual passholders. For an additional $50, you can buy a second membership for your spouse or partner.

Some Specialized Dining Plan Vocabulary

Advance Dining Reservations (ADRs) are highly recommended, and in many (if not *most* cases) they are essential. The best restaurants, character meals, and dinner shows fill up very quickly. If you have a particular favorite or prefer to eat at a certain time, make *all* of your reservations six months ahead of time. (And before you do that, read "Tremendous Tip #1" in chapter 16 before you book. It will help you maximize your chances to score hard-to-get reservations.) There's really no way around this. Luckily, reservations are fairly straightforward to make online, especially if the restaurant isn't one of the most popular venues or you're going to be there in the off season. Just use the My Disney Experience App, find the restaurant where you want to eat, and click on Find a Table. You'll be asked for the number in your party and can then enter a specific time when you'd like to eat. If that exact time isn't available, times as close as possible to your first choice will be offered. If you find an acceptable time, click to accept that reservation. The My Disney Experience App is intuitive and pretty easy to navigate. Before your trip, become familiar with how it works.

It's also possible to call (407) WDW-DINE or (407) 939-3463 and make your meal reservation that way. Speaking directly, politely, and persuasively to a cast member might (in some cases) get you a coveted reservation opening before it's even offered online. Another useful tactic is to check with popular restaurants either online or by phone a day or two before you hope to dine there in an attempt to scoop up a recent cancellation. There are no guarantees that this will work, however.

Once you make an ADR at a particular restaurant for a particular time, you're locked in. This can be a doubled-edged sword. Don't feel like a big, sit-down meal tonight? Sudden change in your plans? If you don't cancel your reservation at least one day in advance, you will be charged $10 *per person in your party*. That can add up pretty quickly, if you're the type who changes plans on the spur of the moment.

Quick-service (counter-service) meals are those where you pay for the food before you eat. (An exception to this rule is the Pepper Market at the Coronado Springs Hotel where you pay as you leave.) The quick-service meal consists of an entrée or a combo meal, and a non-alcoholic beverage or a single serving of beer, wine, or a cocktail. It's like a fast-food restaurant in most ways. You order your food at a counter or select it in a cafeteria, pay for it, take it on a tray to a table, and clear the table when you are finished. No reservations are possible at this type of restaurant. Quality varies widely. Some quick-serve places feature a standard burger, fries, and nuggets ho-hum experience, but others offer eye-opening, tastebud-tickling, pleasant surprises, as you'll soon see. Wait until you try Cookes of Dublin at Disney Springs, Sommerfest at the Germany Pavilion at Epcot, or those luscious lobster rolls at Columbia Harbour House at the Magic Kingdom!

Table-service (full-service) meals means you are seated by a host/hostess and have at least some portion of your meal brought to your table by a server. A buffet meal is still considered a table-service meal since your server brings your drinks and the table is cleared after you leave. In most cases, you'll want to reserve a table well in advance to avoid disappointment. Prime times go very quickly, as do the very popular character meals. Some table-service restaurants are located at the various resort hotels, while others are found in the theme parks and Disney Springs. Character meals are always table-service meals, as are casual, unique/themed, and fine/signature meals.

Casual meals are those where you are seated by a host/hostess and receive full service by a member of the wait staff. The food will be decent and sometimes better than that, and it will not be too expensive. In a lot of ways, your experience at a casual place would be similar to what is available back home in many medium-sized communities. Examples include Tony's Town Square on Main Street, U.S.A., Big River Grill and Brewing Works on the BoardWalk, and the ABC Commissary at Hollywood Studios. Quality varies, but there are plenty of good choices.

Unique/themed meals accept reservations. Your dining experience at one of these places is definitely going to be special because of the unusual décor and the types of foods available. This is an experience you would be unlikely to have anywhere else but at a Disney property. Examples are Tusker House at the Animal Kingdom, the Sci-Fi Dine-in Theatre Restaurant at Hollywood Studios, 'Ohana at the Polynesian Village Resort, and Raglan Road Irish Pub and Restaurant at Disney Springs. At least one (if not several) of your meals while on vacation at Walt Disney World should be at a unique/themed restaurant.

Fine/signature meals are la crème de la crème, the top of the heap, the point of the pinnacle...well, you get the idea. They will set you back *two* table service meal credits on the Disney Dining Plan. You are highly advised to book your table six months in advance at the very hottest of the hot tickets such as Flying Fish on the BoardWalk or Le Cellier Steakhouse in the Canada Pavilion at Epcot. At some, like Victoria & Albert's at the Grand Floridian, you'll find out how it feels to be a royal. The service, food, wine, and entire experience is superb, but the V & A is not on any Disney Dining Plan. You'll pay out-of-pocket there, and it's *very* expensive. A meal at Morimoto Asia, that's *Iron Chef* Morimoto, at Disney Springs; Cinderella's Royal Table in Fantasyland at the Magic Kingdom; Tiffins at the Animal Kingdom; the Hollywood Brown Derby at Hollywood Studios or at any of the other fine/signature restaurants is a pleasure you won't soon forget. It's the kind of experience that makes a celebration special and can make your vacation at Walt Disney World even more memorable.

Snacks are extremely varied and can be identified, for purposes of the Disney Dining Plan, by their small, purple-and-white checkerboard icon. Muffins, individual pieces of fruit, bagels, bottles of water, ice cream treats, an individual box of popcorn, a side-dish in a quick-service restaurant such as a cup of soup, a 20 ounce carbonated beverage, a 12 ounce cup of coffee or tea...the list is practically endless. Lots of emphasis on healthier eating habits means you can now count carrot sticks, apple slices, corn on the cob, a baked potato, or hummus with pita bread as a snack, too.

Refillable resort mugs, also called rapid-fill mugs, are provided for each member of your party over three years of age if you are on any of the Disney dining plans. The colorful mugs are insulated but *not* microwaveable and *not* dishwasher safe. Each holds about 16 fluid ounces. (Guests who are not on the meal plans can purchase the mugs; in that case, the cost is a flat $17.99 for the length of your stay, no matter how long or short your stay is.) Coffee, tea, hot chocolate, and Coke products—even Hi-C and Powerade at certain refill stations but *not* milk or fruit juice—are the beverages intended for use in these mugs. Water is always free. You can't fill the mugs inside the theme parks, but they are good for use at *any* Disney resort hotel, regardless of the one where you happen to be staying.

What if you're switching from coffee in the morning to a Coke following an afternoon swim? Look for the mug wash stations located where you refill your mug. Each mug has an RFID bar code that will deactivate it after your stay at a Disney Resort is over. Don't put it through the dishwasher at your deluxe villa if you have one, however—that will render the chip useless!

Disney's Healthy Living Initiative is intended to make eating healthier possible, even on a Walt Disney World vacation. On menus, you can identify healthier options for kids' meals by the Mickey Check icon. Lower in sodium, sugar, and trans fats, these choices provide a way to help parents encourage healthy eating habits. Instead of the usual fish and chips, pizza, mac and cheese, or fried chicken tenders sided with fries, you'll find options like grilled fish or chicken skewers, steamed veggies, and fruit, for example. Small servings of low-fat milk are also available. Thanks to Disney's Healthy Living Initiative, if adults don't want a dessert at a table-service meal, they are allowed to substitute a side salad, fruit plate, or cup of soup instead. Nice!

Trades can be made on the dining plans. One single credit for a quick-service meal can be traded for three snacks, as long as the trade is completed in a single transaction. Say you want a muffin, a banana, and a cup of coffee for breakfast. Those three snack items taken together count as one quick-service meal credit.

Pizza delivery service is available for guests on the Disney Dining Plan staying at any of Disney's All-Star Resorts, Caribbean Beach, Pop Century, and at both Port Orleans Riverside and French Quarter. Two adult meal credits will provide a pizza entrée, two non-alcoholic beverages, and two desserts. Gratuity is included, so no tipping is expected.

Private in-room dining is pricey. You'll be charged *two* credits for just one meal. Gratuity is included. At lunch and dinner, you'll get an entrée, dessert, and beverage (specialty drinks or alcoholic beverages such as beer, wine, or cocktails).

Credits, sometimes called entitlements, are the basic currency of your Disney Dining Plan. You spend them throughout your visit until they run out. It doesn't matter if you spend them all in the first few days or spread them out over many days. Your MagicBand keeps track of your totals, so monitor it as you go. More elaborate meals at fine/signature restaurants, the three dinner shows, and any of the many character meals are more costly than quick-service options.

All credits are not created equal. There are table-service credits, quick-service credits, and snack credits. A credit has no set value. You could spend table-service credits at inexpensive counter-service restaurants and order the least expensive items on the menu. Or, you could spend your credits at a Disney fine/signature restaurant and order the most expensive items. In the first case, you won't get a good return on your financial investment. In the second case, you will.

Out-of-pocket food or drink expenses are those not covered by your Disney Dining Plan. Gratuities not already covered by the plan, beverages served in souvenir cups, any food purchases made for children under three, food purchases made after all of your meal credits have been spent, or meals at restaurants not participating in the dining plan must all be paid for by you at the time you make the purchase, either by using cash, a credit card, or a Disney gift card.

Dinner shows can be an enjoyable part of your vacation. The meals are served family-style and feature live entertainment. Any dinner show requires advance reservations. Gratuities are included, so there is no need to tip additionally unless you've ordered items not part of the package. The Western-style Hoop-Dee-Doo Musical Revue is located at Disney's Fort Wilderness Resort & Campground. The Spirit of Aloha Dinner Show including hula and fire dancing takes place at Disney's Polynesian Village Resort. Mickey's Backyard BBQ is set outdoors under a covered pavilion next to the Campsites at Disney's Fort Wilderness. The BBQ is a country-style hoedown with line dancing, a country-western band, and fancy rope tricks. The cost for a dinner show is two credits. Disney quick-service dining plan credits cannot be used for a dinner show.

Character meals are often the highlight of any Disney vacation, especially (but by no means only) for younger children. Dining with their animated friends come to life is magical. Although that word is often overused in official Disney literature, in this case it's entirely accurate. This is the perfect chance for your family members to interact individually with costumed characters, all of whom will spend time at your table posing for photos and signing autographs. Don't be shy about attending a character meal if you are a solo adult, a couple, or all-adult group, either. They are great for guests of any age. There are many of these delightful meals available, each of which will be explained in detail later. Currently, the most difficult character meal reservation to obtain is Cinderella's Royal Table in Cinderella Castle at the Magic Kingdom. It's also one of the most expensive, costing *two* meal credits, but gratuity is included. In effect, you pay for two meals and eat one. Still, for little girls and their families, the experience is priceless.

Disney signature restaurants are those special dining experiences that keep you coming back year after year to Walt Disney World. Because their cost is significantly higher than average, you'll need to use *two* full-service meal credits. Dress is "resort casual" in most of these lovely establishments. Make every attempt to book reservations six months in advance.

Restaurants participating as a part of the Disney Dining Plan vary from year to year. Some are added, while others opt out. Check early in the year of your visit to see a listing of those restaurants that will accept your credits. At press time, participating signature restaurants include:

- Artist Point at Disney's Wilderness Lodge
- BOATHOUSE at Disney Springs
- California Grill at Disney's Contemporary Resort
- Cítricos and Cítricos Chef's Domain at Disney's Grand Floridian Hotel & Spa
- Flying Fish Café at Disney's BoardWalk
- Hollywood Brown Derby at Disney's Hollywood Studios
- Jiko—The Cooking Place at Disney's Animal Kingdom Lodge
- Le Cellier Steakhouse at the Canada Pavilion at Epcot
- Monsieur Paul at the France Pavilion at Epcot
- Morimoto Asia at Disney Springs
- Narcoossee's at Disney's Grand Floridian Hotel & Spa
- Paddlefish at Disney Springs
- STK Orlando at Disney Springs
- Tiffins at Animal Kingdom
- Victoria & Albert's
- Yachtsman Steakhouse at Disney's Yacht Club

Victoria & Albert's at the Grand Floridian is *not* on the list of Disney Dining Plan participating restaurants. While it's definitely a fine/signature restaurant, you'll need to pay out-of-pocket to eat there. The dress code is more "dressy," too. Men are expected to wear a sport coat and slacks, and ladies should wear dresses, suits, pants suits, blouse and skirt, or something other than what they've been wearing traipsing around Epcot or the Animal Kingdom all day. If men don't have a sport coat, they can usually be accommodated by the staff since they have a number of these in assorted sizes on hand. Many of those who dine there do so on expense accounts.

A Few Key Restrictions

All guests staying in a room or suite must be on the *same* dining plan. You can't have the children on the quick-service plan while you and your spouse purchase the regular plan and Grandpa and Grandma choose the deluxe plan. That simply won't fly. Everyone must be on the *same* plan or everyone must be on no plan at all, if that's what you ultimately decide. Not only must you all be on the same plan, you must all purchase the plan for exactly the same number of nights that you will be staying in the resort hotel. It's an all-or-nothing proposition. You can't decide to forgo the dining plan for the first and last nights of your stay, for example, or extend the dining plan for days on either end of your visit when you aren't staying at a Disney hotel. You can't try it for a few days and then decide to drop it—*unless* you are splitting your stay between two Disney hotels, that is. In that case, you might decide to try the plan while staying at one hotel and try paying for meals and snacks out-of-pocket at the other to see which way you prefer.

Disney no longer allows guests to "double book" dinner reservations. For example, your party can't book both Cinderella's Royal Table *and* Be Our Guest for lunch at noon on June 8. What you *can* do, however, is book your reservations *two hours* apart. That, the system *will* allow. In this way, you may book Cinderella at 11:30 and Be Our Guest at 1:30 if you want the ability to make up your mind the day before. Don't forget, however, that you'll be charged a $10 per person fee if you forget to cancel a reservation less than 24 hours ahead of time!

As if this wasn't complicated enough already, as of 2018 there are three possible dining plans from which to choose. Prices change frequently and without notice. In fact, since I began writing this guide, they have risen and had to be updated below, so do confirm the latest prices online before your trip.

Three Disney Dining Plans

For the purpose of calculating dining plan costs, Disney decrees that children become "adults" at the age of ten. A child must be between 3–9 years old to qualify for the lower "child" rate.

Quick-Service Dining

- Two quick-service meals for each day of your stay: an entrée *or* a combo meal (such as a hamburger and fries, fish and chips, etc.) if available, and a beverage such as regular drinks (milk, coffee, tea, carbonated drinks, juices) as well as non-alcoholic specialty drinks (if available) and beer, wine, and cocktails for those over 21 years of age.

- Two snacks per day.
- One refillable resort mug.
- Cost per day: adult $52.49, child $21.75.

Regular Dining

- One quick-service meal for each day of your stay: an entrée *or* a combo meal if available, and a beverage such as non-alcoholic specialty drink (if available) and beer, wine and cocktails for those over 21.
- One table-service meal per day: an entrée, a dessert, and a beverage such as non-alcoholic specialty drinks (if available) and beer, wine and cocktails for those over 21 *or* one full buffet meal.
- Two snacks per day.
- One refillable resort mug.
- Cost per day: adult $75.49, child $25.80.

Deluxe Dining

- Three complete meals for each day of your stay in any combination your choose. You may opt for three full-service sit-down meals every single day if you'd like, or you may choose any combination of full-service and quick-service meals, including full buffet meals. All meals on the Deluxe Dining Plan include non-alcoholic specialty drinks (if available) and beer, wine, and cocktails.
- Two snacks per day.
- One refillable resort mug.
- Cost per day: adults $116.24, child $39.90.

If you need information and can't wait, call 407 WDW-DINE (407 939-3463). You may also ask your question by email sent to guest.mail@wdw.disneyonline.com.

The Free Disney Dining Plan

Yes, you heard right! At selected dates from July or August through December, Walt Disney Word will offer the regular dining plan for "free" to its guests staying at the Disney resort hotels. (You could pay to upgrade the plan to deluxe if you're so inclined.) There's one caveat, though, and it's a big one. If you sign up for the free dining plan, you are not eligible to qualify for any discounted promotions for your room or on the price for admission tickets to the park. If you aren't getting any discount on your room or tickets, then it's a great deal, of course. But most people find that the discounts they can qualify for on accommodations and park admission tickets will offset any savings the free Disney Dining Plan would provide. If your party is relatively small and you like to stay at the deluxe hotels, it's doubtful you'd save money with this offer. It might make sense for a large group staying at a value hotel, though.

So, there you have it—the basics of the Disney dining plans. Let me assure you that it not only sounds complicated, it *is* complicated. My best advice? Those of you who are intrigued by the plan and think that the ease of pre-paying for meals is attractive ought to give it a try. You might want to start with the regular plan. You'll get to sample the snacks, grab one quick-service meal, and have one nice, sit-down, table-service meal every day. By the end of your visit, you should have a good idea of whether or not the dining plan made sense for your family.

If you're anything like most folks, you'll be spending plenty of cash eating at Walt Disney World no matter how you do it. Comestibles are costly, in most cases considerably more costly than the very same things would be off-site. Many guests are shocked by this fact, so prepare yourself for it ahead of time. Expect to pay a hefty premium, as much as a third more, for the considerable convenience of dining while you're on Disney property. Some meals are well worth it, others not nearly so much. We'll get to all of that in the chapters to come.

For now, take a little time to review the pluses and minuses of participating in a Disney Dining Plan; talk it over with the other members in your group. You have just two ways to go. Either take a leap of faith and try out one of the dining plans that best suits your needs and your budget or see how much you spend eating on your vacation *without* the dining plan and calculate whether it could have actually saved you any money or not—and that requires a lot of keeping track of every food purchase.

As I said at the beginning of this chapter, there are those who swear by the merits of the Disney Dining Plan and couldn't imagine a Walt Disney World vacation without it, just as there are others who've tried it once and said every bit as adamantly *never again*. The choice is all yours. No matter which way you select, it's hard to go too far wrong while dining at Walt Disney World.

About the Dining Reviews

In the following chapters, I indicate the cost of eating at each Disney quick-service or table-service restaurant with a range of prices:

*	$14.99 and lower
**	$15-$34.99
***	$35-$59.99
****	$60 and higher

Depending on how finicky you are, you can enjoy a good meal at the low end of the range or splurge on the high. Of course, Disney frequently changes its prices—usually upwards—so if cost is a crucial factor in your decision to eat at a specific restaurant, check the menu beforehand. For up-to-the-minute, guaranteed accurate information, you should check only the menus on the official Walt Disney World website. Use the menus cribbed on Disney fan sites with caution.

Unless otherwise indicated, the cost range is per adult. If the restaurant offers a Tables in Wonderland discount, you'll see the designation "TiW" after the cost range.

The credit "cost" for each meal is designated with "S" (Snack), "Q" (Quick Service), or "T" (Table Service), depending upon what kind of Disney Dining Plan (DDP) credit it requires.

Reservations are *always* recommended at table-service restaurants. At the more popular ones, like Cinderella's Royal Table, 'Ohana, and Chef Mickey's, reservations might as well be *required*, as they're snapped up quickly. (At some venues, like Disney's dinner shows, reservations really *are* required.)

During less busy seasons, you might get lucky as a walk-up and score a table. It never hurts to try. But if you know your dining plans in advance, avoid possible disappointment and book a reservation.

The dining reviews are ordered by DDP credit type—snack, quick service, table service—and then alphabetically within each of those categories. Usually, there are snack items available at locations designated as accepting quick-service credits, so when you see a venue designated as "quick service", assume that you can use snack credits there, too, for some items. In contrast, table-service locations rarely if ever have snack items available. Food kiosks and stores that sell food items, whether eligible for the dining plan or not, are organized at the start of each section. A few venues are not on the dining plan; their reviews are placed wherever it makes sense to put them.

It's like reading a manufacturer's warranty, isn't it? I don't know about you, but I've built up an appetite...

Magic Kingdom, Part One

Main Street, U.S.A,
Adventureland, and Frontierland

If you're like most guests, this is the one theme park you'll definitely want to visit during your Walt Disney World vacation. Whether you're the youngest child or the most senior member of the group, you'll find the Magic Kingdom is the place where dreams really do come true.

This Disney theme park, the first one to open on October 1, 1971, is well-organized and loaded with places where you can grab something tasty on the go, sit down for a quick bite for lunch, or enjoy a leisurely dinner after a big day of fun. First, we will consider where to find what you'd like to eat on Main Street, U.S.A., followed by Adventureland, Frontierland, Liberty Square, Fantasyland, and Tomorrowland. That way, you can easily turn to the section in this guide where you happen to be at any given time and check out the food and beverage offerings you'll find there. You can also take a finger-walking "tour" in the pages of this book through each theme park well before your arrival to determine when and where you'd like to make those key dining reservations. We'll tour clockwise through the park.

Walt Disney World now makes every effort to accommodate special dietary needs and food allergies. Kosher, low fat, low sodium, sugar free, gluten free, vegan, vegetarian, and other special diet menus are currently available, but be sure to ask (preferably in advance of your arrival) and then confirm again with your server. Several of these choices are noted on the menus. Times have changed, and healthy alternatives now play a major role in dining options.

Main Street, U.S.A.

Walt Disney intended Main Street to represent a typical, small American town at the turn of the last century from 1900 to about 1910. It's based on a combination of three towns: Marceline, Missouri, where Walt spent a happy part of his growing-up years; the Henry Ford Museum and Greenfield Village, also called the Edison Institute, in Dearborn, Michigan; and Ft. Collins, Colorado, where Harper Goff, principal designer of the original Main Street in Disneyland, grew up. It will also look familiar if you've seen *Lady and the Tramp*, since it's an echo of Lady's hometown, too. At Walt Disney World, however, the area was changed to represent not just Midwestern America but other areas of the country as well, including New England. In fact, if you look closely, you'll see that each of the buildings in the middle of Main Street in the area known as the Four Corners is done in a different architectural style. You might not notice it, but Main Street is paved with resilient asphalt to make walking less fatiguing for tired feet.

Walt Disney said

> For those of us who remember the carefree time it re-creates, Main Street will bring back happy memories. For younger visitors, it is an adventure in turning back the calendar to the days of their grandfather's youth.

For kids today, it's more like a look back at great-great-grandma and grandpa's childhood years.

Main Street, U.S.A. Kiosks, Wagons, and Carts

Stop by the Main Street Ice Cold Refreshment Stand near the central hub on your way to the castle for fresh fruit, cold drinks, and various snacks. There is usually an ice cream cart parked in front of the Town Square Theatre that also has frozen bananas and Olaf lemonade-strawberry bars. Look for a permanent ice cream stand on the left side of the hub facing the castle for pretzels, churros, cotton candy, frozen bananas, glazed almonds, and frozen fruit bars—oh, yes, and Mickey ice cream bars and ice cream sandwiches, too!

There are popcorn carts located on Main Street and throughout the park. The smell is irresistible—you can always share a warm box of popcorn as you stroll down the street. More than five million boxes are sold here every year. You will also find refillable souvenir buckets if you just can't get enough. Try not to spill! Popcorn is the bane of those busy sweepers.

Note: Because you can count on finding bottles of Dasani water being sold at just about any kiosk, wagon, cart, or counter, I won't specifically mention it again. A bottle of Dasani water costs one snack credit if you're on the Disney Dining Plan.

Main Street Confectionery

On the right corner as you're facing the castle and just across Town Square, you'll find this sweet shop filled with character-themed treats. Employees are able to make creative suggestions, and the results are delightful. Try Mickey-shaped Rice Krispie treats with ears dipped in chocolate or a caramel chocolate-covered apple that looks like Mickey's famous red shorts. Everything to satisfy your sweet tooth is on colorful display here. Watch the action in the back of the store as cast members make cotton candy, peanut brittle, fudge, and caramel apples.

Plaza Ice Cream Parlor

DDP: No / Cost: $
TYPE: American; Quick Service; Snacks

At the end of Main Street on the right, this turn-of-the-twentieth-century gem offers hand-scooped ice cream treats. You can get a single scoop, sugar-free sorbet, or decadent waffle-bowl ice cream sundae. Top your treat with hot fudge, peanut butter, or caramel. Fat-free treats are available, too.

Casey's Corner

DDP: One credit (Q) / Cost: $
TYPE: American; Quick Service; Lunch and Dinner

Inspired by the All-American pastime, the famous 1888 poem by Ernest Thayer, and the Disney cartoon from 1946, this spot has a "Casey at the Bat" ballpark theme. Craving a foot-long chili-cheese dog? Some addictive corn dog nuggets? Pulled pork on a barbecue slaw dog? You'll find them and more at Casey's Corner, a red, white, and blue quick-service restaurant on the left side of Main Street facing the castle and adjacent to the hub.

Listen to the pianist tickle the ivories playing old-time tunes and relax with a selection of hot dogs, fries, brownies, cotton candy, Cracker Jack, and everything else kids (or adults!) might desire. No Mickey Check meals here. No carrot sticks or yogurt substitutions, but you *can* get apple slices instead of fries. Casey's is all things indulgent when you feel like swinging for the bleachers with a calorie splurge that might hit a home run.

Main Street Bakery

DDP: One credit (Q) / Cost: $
TYPE: American; Quick Service; Snacks

If you're missing your Starbuck's favorites, be it frappuccino, espresso, latte, smoothie, iced coffee, or hot chocolate, don't worry—you'll find them all here. The bakery is on the right side of the street just past the Four Corners. Add delicious Disney baked goods or pastries from La Boulange for a snack or quick breakfast. The bakery also serves ham, egg, and Swiss croissant sandwiches; a spinach, feta, and egg-white wrap; and bacon, egg, and Gouda or sausage, egg, and cheddar sandwiches. What you *won't* find here nowadays are the ever-popular giant, gooey cinnamon rolls. Look for them instead at Gaston's Tavern in Fantasyland.

Crystal Palace

DDP: One credit (T) / Cost: $$-$$$ (TiW)
TYPE: American; Character Buffet; Breakfast, Lunch, and Dinner

Past Casey's heading toward Adventureland is one of the prettiest dining spots in the Magic Kingdom. One of the most delightful aspects of dining here is being joined table-side by friends from the Hundred Acre Wood: Winnie the Pooh, Tigger, Piglet, and Eeyore.

Having a meal at the Crystal Palace is like dining in a Victorian glass conservatory. Ceilings soar, white walls are covered with decorative architectural embellishments, and lush greenery adds to the period authenticity. Meals are served buffet style. Breakfast offers made-to-order omelettes, bacon and eggs, Mickey waffles, cereals, fresh fruit, breads and pastries, and just about any breakfast item you can imagine. Lunch and dinner include salads, soups and breads, carved meats, fish, chicken, vegetable creations, peel-and-eat shrimp, and house-made sweets and ice cream. You won't leave this "palace" hungry.

The Plaza Restaurant

DDP: One credit (T) / Cost: $$ (TiW)
TYPE: American; Casual; Lunch and Dinner

Just past the ice cream parlor on your right at the end of Main Street and facing Cinderella Castle, you'll find this quintessential American restaurant that offers something sure to please most members of your party. Walls of mirrors, wrought-iron chairs, and a 1900s ambience make the Plaza a welcome respite where you can regroup while enjoying appetizers like wedge salad, loaded fries, or seasonal soups. Entrées remind you of home cooking: meat loaf, chicken, cheese steak, tuna, or fried green tomato sandwiches; brisket, vegetable, or Angus burgers; and chicken with strawberries salad. Any room left for dessert? Try one of the many fountain specialties including milk shakes, cakes, or a slice of caramel apple pie à la mode. Prices are the same at lunch and dinner.

Tony's Town Square Restaurant

DDP: One credit (T) / Cost: $$ (TiW)
TYPE: Italian; Casual; Lunch and Dinner

This pretty little Italian-American restaurant is filled with light from its many windows and has lacy, wrought-iron chairs and pots of hanging ferns. Dine on the outdoor terrace and you'll look right onto Main Street, so there's always plenty to watch as you wait for your meal to arrive. If it looks familiar, that's because it's based on Tony's trattoria from *Lady and the Tramp*, the one where the canine sweethearts shared a plate of spaghetti—and a kiss.

You'll find traditional Italian appetizers like Caprese salads, meats and cheeses, pasta fagioli soup, and calamari, entrées such as chicken parmigiana, rigatoni, spaghetti, shrimp scampi, pizza, and American favorites like steak. Tony's features Italian specialty desserts such as tiramisù, gelato, cannoli, and a rich chocolate layer cake that's pretty spectacular. There's a nice Italian wine selection from Umbria, Veneto, and Tuscany as well as Birra Moretti Lager. Prices don't drop at lunch.

Adventureland

Leaving the Crystal Palace behind, you'll cross a short bridge and then see in front of you the entrance to Adventureland. You'll find yourself surrounded by luxuriant jungle foliage and a wild, exciting, tropical atmosphere. The area is further divided into an Arabian Village section and the Caribbean Plaza. You'll note plenty of Polynesian influences in the carved Tikis, masks, and decorative wooden poles. When he opened Disneyland in 1955, Walt Disney's concept of Adventureland was strongly influenced by the 1951 Bogart/Hepburn film, *The African Queen*. Walt said:

> To create a land that would make this dream reality, we pictured ourselves far from civilization, in the remote jungles of Asia and Africa.

In Orlando, the concept has been expanded even further.

Adventureland Kiosks, Wagons and Carts

Miles from the usual park fare, there's an egg roll (veggie or pork) wagon that also sells cheeseburger spring rolls (sometimes), corn dog nuggets, and chocolate chip cookies during busy seasons.

Another treat open during busy times at the park is the Adventureland nut cart near the Jungle Cruise where you'll find glazed almonds, ice-cream, and frozen treats.

The Adventureland popcorn cart offers a welcome snack for busy guests on the go. Check for the purple-and-white checkerboard snack icon if you're on the Disney Dining Plan.

Sunshine Tree Terrace

DDP: No / Cost: $
TYPE: American; Quick Service; Snacks

Just over the bridge on your way into Adventureland, you'll find the towering Swiss Family Robinson Treehouse, and with it, the Sunshine Tree Terrace. Citrus swirl, soft serve vanilla ice cream, a refreshing raspberry-lemonade slush, and lots of kinds of cool drinks will be a welcome break on a warm, steamy, Florida day.

Aloha Isle

DDP: One credit (S) / Cost: $
TYPE: American; Quick Service; Snacks

If you've never tried the immensely popular pineapple Dole Whip cup or float, here's your chance. Look for it behind the Enchanted Tiki Room. This unique, addictive snack is relatively low in fat and calories, gluten-free, vegan, and non-dairy. This is true even if you get the pineapple/vanilla swirl version. Indulge in this refreshing and delicious snack without guilt! Fresh pineapple spears and pineapple juice are also served here.

Tortuga Tavern

DDP: One credit (Q) / Cost: $
TYPE: Southwestern/Mexican; Quick service; Lunch and Dinner

Count yourself lucky if Tortuga Tavern is open when you happen to visit Adventureland because it's often closed. During slower days in the park, you'll find turkey legs or a hot dog and chips combo plus chocolate chip cookies and fountain beverages. The tavern is usually only open during times when the Magic Kingdom is exceptionally busy. It's a great spot for delicious barbecue sandwiches. The cuisine is Mexican with *mucho* emphasis on the spicy and hearty, but there's also a roasted corn and vegetable salad with red wine vinaigrette for those with tamer palates and lighter appetites. Nutritious Mickey Check meals are served and there's a kid's mac and cheese option. Grab a chocolate chip cookie for dessert, and you'll be ready to take a voyage on the Pirates of the Caribbean attraction, which is located just across the walkway from Tortuga Tavern.

Jungle Navigation Co. Ltd. Skipper Canteen

DDP: One credit (T) / Cost: $$ (TiW)
TYPE: African/Asian/Latin; Casual; Lunch and Dinner

One of the newer Magic Kingdom restaurants (2016), the Skipper Canteen is one of the first buildings you'll see on your right as you enter Adventureland. It boasts three differently themed dining rooms: the Falls Family Parlor, the S.E.A. Room, and the largest of the three, the Mess Hall. Skipper Canteen attempts to capture all the rollicking, wild fun of the Jungle Cruise attraction.

You'll see that influence in the menu titles: Falls Family Falafel, Ginger's "Croc" of Hot and Sour Soup, and Orinoco Ida's Cachapas (corn pancakes). It provides adventurous new African, Asian, and Latin flavors as well as several unique entrées, even for those "well-seasoned" guests who've visited the Magic Kingdom many times. If some of those in your group prefer a slightly tamer dining experience, don't worry. There are plenty of American-style choices on the menu, too. Pork, steak, curried vegetable stew, whole fried fish, lamb chops, beefy baked pasta, and heads-on shrimp are featured.

Desserts like Quick Sand (jasmine rice pudding, mango sauce, hibiscus meringue, lemon curd, and pineapple) or Kangaloosh (African-inspired chocolate cake with caramelized bananas, caramel-cashew ice cream and topped with coffee dust) are just two of the sure-to-please sweets at this walk-on-the-wild-side Magic Kingdom culinary experience.

Frontierland

Continue through Adventureland and you'll find yourself in the rootin', tootin' old West back when living on the frontier meant wide-open spaces and facing down danger on all sides.

When Frontierland opened in Disneyland in 1955, Walt Disney explained it this way:

> It is here that we experience the story of our country's past. The color, romance and drama of frontier America as it developed from wilderness trails to roads, riverboats, railroads and civilization. A tribute to the faith, courage and ingenuity of our hearty pioneers who blaze the trails and made this progress possible.

Fictional Tom Sawyer and Huck Finn grew up in Hannibal, Missouri, while Walt and his brother Roy explored the rural environs of Marceline, Missouri, but kids from everywhere will appreciate the good times to be had in Frontierland. Modern sensibilities are perhaps somewhat less likely to be fascinated with this particular historical period as people were sixty-plus years ago when Walt spoke those words, but you'll find a few satisfying dining opportunities when your party is ready to take a break from the attractions, both wild and tame.

Frontierland Kiosks, Wagons, and Carts

Not really looking for a meal but definitely looking for *something*? Winding your way through Frontierland, you'll find three snack carts chock full of appealing items. Churros are long, thin donuts, Mexican style. You'll smell them before you see them! During busy seasons, turkey legs are offered by one cart and hot dogs by yet another. Look for popcorn and ice cream carts along the walkways. These carts make it easy for your group to catch up with some calories as you mosey through Frontierland.

Prairie Outpost

This sweet shop is worth a visit, but it might take some hunting to find (it's next to Pecos Bill). It's well stocked with chocolate-dipped pretzels, lollipops of many kinds, a colorful spectrum of jelly bellies, hand-made chocolate candies, and Disney-style sweets available in pretty souvenir containers to take to teachers, family, or friends back home.

Westward Ho Refreshments

DDP: No / Cost: $
TYPE: American; Quick Service; Snacks

Across from Pecos Bill on your way to Big Thunder Mountain Railroad, you will find this simple kiosk that resembles a rustic cabin. In season, corn dogs are on the menu. Hot and cold beverages, fountain drinks, chips, muffins, and chocolate chip cookies are available.

Golden Oak Outpost

DDP: One credit (S) / Cost: $
TYPE: American; Quick Service; Snacks

Near Splash Mountain, this cozy Western counter is open *only* during busy seasons and some weekends. Fare is very basic: chicken nuggets, waffle fries, chocolate chip cookies, fountain beverages, and frozen lemonade.

Pecos Bill Tall Tale Inn and Café

DDP: One credit (Q) / Cost: $
TYPE: Southwestern/Mexican; Quick Service; Lunch and Dinner

Feel free to rustle up some rib-stickin' grub with a decidedly Southwestern influence in this casual dining establishment, justly famous for its *huge* help-yourself toppings bar. Burgers, fajitas, taco salads, burritos, and loaded nachos are the main courses. There is a Mickey Check meal for kids with Smucker's Uncrustables as well as standard kids meals with mini-corn dogs or mac and cheese. Lots of beverage choices are on hand. Desserts include red velvet or sometimes tres leches cake, churros, and Greek yogurt. Find seating indoors or out.

The Diamond Horseshoe

DDP: One credit (T) / Cost: $$
TYPE: American; Casual; Lunch and Dinner

You'll find the Horseshoe next door to the Liberty Tree Tavern. It's the first restaurant on the border between Frontierland and Liberty Square. Like several other dining venues in this area, Diamond Horseshoe is open during *very* busy times of the year, like the Thanksgiving and Christmas holidays, and some weekends. There's a player piano on the stage that doesn't— play, that is. Most recently, the menu has been an all-you-care-to-enjoy meal with salad and cornbread, pulled pork, ham, beef, turkey, sausage, "cowboy" beans, baked mac and cheese, corn on the cob, and "campfire" brownies for dessert, which means brownies with toasted marshmallow cream on top. Lunch and dinner are priced the same.

You're going to do more than eat and drink while you're visiting Walt Disney World, and getting through even half of the Magic Kingdom in a day will leave your schedule jam-packed. If you're planning to see it all in a single day, a definite possibility if you plan very carefully, turn the page and you'll find dining and snacking choices to enjoy while your party heads for the second half of the park. If you're splitting your Magic Kingdom visit over two days (or more), get a good rest tonight and you'll be ready for a hearty breakfast in the morning.

Magic Kingdom, Part Two
Liberty Square, Fantasyland, and Tomorrowland

Liberty Square

Way back in the early 1950s when Disneyland was still just a dream, Walt hoped to include a nod to early American history off Main Street, U.S.A. That didn't happen in Anaheim, but as the country's bicentennial birthday and Walt Disney World was in the planning stages, Walt's idea became Liberty Square. Flags of the thirteen original colonies are proudly flown here. You'll see many authentic colonial-period antiques on display. A bell made from the same mold as the original Liberty Bell was cast in 1989 and brought to Liberty Square. The Liberty Tree, originally an elm, that played such a prominent role in Boston's early history (and in Walt Disney's film *Johnny Tremaine*) was honored when a hundred-year-old oak found on the property was transplanted to the area. A younger oak then was grafted to the original tree. Look for the two lanterns signaling "two if by sea," just as Paul Revere once did, except that in Liberty Square, they're visible in the upper window of a replica of Philadelphia's House of Burgesses instead of the old North Church.

Liberty Square Kiosks, Wagons and Carts

On busy days, a small kiosk selling cheese pizza will be open. A popcorn and an ice cream cart are usually available.

Some different, healthy choices are found at the Liberty Square Market. Try corn on the cob loaded with spices, or a baked potato. Fresh grape tomatoes and lots of fresh fruit is on tempting display. Seating is available at tables, some of it shaded. You may not even need lunch afterward!

Sleepy Hollow

DDP: One credit (S) / Cost: $
TYPE: American; Quick Service; Snacks

Many things on this inventive menu aren't available elsewhere in the park. You'll find Sleepy Hollow as you leave Liberty Square on the way to Cinderella Castle. Satisfy your hunger with a big sausage-and-cheddar-stuffed pretzel, sweet-and-spicy chicken waffle, funnel cake topped with seasonal ice cream flavors, made-to-order ice cream cookie sandwiches, or Belgian waffles topped with strawberries and whipped cream. Other goodies include a fresh fruit waffle sandwich with chocolate spread, breakfast egg and cheese waffle, baked potato, or hand-dipped corn dog. There are lots of beverage choices on hand, too.

Columbia Harbour House

DDP: One credit (Q) / Cost: $
TYPE: American; Quick Service; Lunch and Dinner

Lobster rolls are the big draw here, and you'll hear guests raving about them. If you're a lobster fan, stop by. It's just down the walkway that leads to the Haunted Mansion. Two other hearty sandwiches are an all-white tuna and a hummus with tomato and broccoli slaw, both with chips. Mickey Check meals for kids feature all-white tuna sandwiches, Smucker's Uncrustables, or a salad with chicken. Three other kids options are chicken nuggets, chicken *and* fish nuggets, or mac and cheese. You can order soups, salads, and sides like corn cobbette, couscous, broccoli, or fries. An adult entrée, "By Land or Sea," features shrimp, salmon, and chicken prepared a number of different ways. Cake, seasonal cobbler, and yogurt round out the bill of fare.

Liberty Tree Tavern

DDP: One credit (T) / Cost: $$ (TiW)
TYPE: American; Casual; Lunch and Dinner

Tucked in right beside the Diamond Horseshoe, you can choose the all-you-care-to-enjoy Patriot's Platter, which comes with family-style servings of turkey, prime rib, pork roast, herbed stuffing, mashed potatoes, vegetables, and mac and cheese. It also comes with a salad and Johnny Appleseed's warm bread pudding topped with vanilla crème anglaise. You can order from an a la carte menu instead if you prefer. Try crab and lobster dip, corn fritters, or clam chowder to start. Entrées are pasta, seared salmon salad, or an Angus cheeseburger. End with some of that yummy bread pudding, sorbet, toffee cake, or—what else?—Boston cream pie. It's like dining in a colonial inn two hundred and fifty years ago.

Fantasyland

For many guests, this is the land that brings back fond memories of childhood favorite stories and characters. The Disneyland version was very dear to Walt Disney's own heart. He said:

> Here is a land of imagination, hopes and dreams. In this timeless land of enchantment the age of chivalry, magic and make-believe are reborn and fairy tales come true. Fantasyland is dedicated to the young and the young at heart, to those who believe that when you wish upon a star your dreams do come true.

When you think of the best-known Disney animated films, Fantasyland is where you'll find them brought to life in family-friendly fashion. Keep in mind, as you plan your visit, that this area gets progressively busier as the day goes on, so come early to avoid long waits.

Fantasyland Kiosks, Wagons, Carts

The new part of Fantasyland features a popcorn cart like no other—it's Maurice's Amazing Popping Machine. It was designed by Belle's father and also serves frozen treats. Hot dogs are only offered from a kiosk in "new" Fantasyland when the park is extremely busy.

The Storybook Circus area has a pretzel stand with melted cheese for pretzel dipping and churros to dip in chocolate sauce. One of the ubiquitous popcorn carts is here, too.

If you want a *different* kind of popcorn snack, try the housemade caramel corn at Big Top Treats. It's made fresh every day. Candy apples, cookies, and (adorable!) fanciful cupcakes shaped like Dumbo and other characters, fresh pineapple, and chocolate-dipped strawberries are featured at Big Top as well.

Prince Eric's Market near the Seven Dwarfs Mine Train has frozen lemonade, a ham-and-cheese pretzel, and (during busy seasons) turkey legs.

Even if you didn't manage to get a reservation at the super-popular Be Our Guest Restaurant, you won't go hungry in Fantasyland!

Cheshire Café

DDP: One credit (S) / Cost: $
TYPE: American; Quick Service; Snacks and Breakfast

Continue walking past Storybook Circus until you see the Mad Tea Party with its spinning teacups. Beside it is this café named for the enigmatic, grinning feline in *Alice in Wonderland*. If you've come early in the day and are looking for a quick, convenient breakfast, look no further. Give that Cheshire Cat Tail a bite—it's a long pastry with pink and purple striped icing. In busy seasons, an assortment of cereals, muffins, whole fruit, juice, coffee (hot or iced), and hot cocoa will hit the spot. Seating is available on a covered patio or at tables under shady umbrellas.

Gaston's Tavern

DDP: One credit (S) / Cost: $
TYPE: American; Quick Service; Lunch and Dinner

Just past Be Our Guest is the he-man-style Gaston's Tavern. Indoor tables can be hard to secure, so have one member of the party save a spot while the rest place the order at the counter. Those famous cinnamon rolls are the big draw here. Gaston also appreciates a good chocolate croissant. Le Fou's Brew is cool in the summer (100% sugar-free frozen apple juice with a touch of toasted marshmallow and mango foam on top) and warm in the winter (hot cocoa with a hint of toasted marshmallow topped with whipped cream and sprinkled with crushed candy cane). You'll also find apples with caramel dip, hummus and chips, veggies and dip, and cups of fruit to round out the snack selection.

Storybook Treats

DDP: One credit (S) / Cost: $
TYPE: American; Quick Service; Snacks

When you're craving something cool and sweet, ice cream at Storybook Treats may be just what you want. Indulge with a hot fudge sundae, a strawberry sundae, a float, or soft-serve ice cream—vanilla, chocolate, or swirl. Lots of cool beverages are available to quench your thirst.

The Friar's Nook

DDP: One credit (Q) / Cost: $
TYPE: American; Quick Service; Lunch and Dinner

Walk through the castle and immediately turn right to find this quick-serve counter. Need a fast snack for the kids or something heartier? Pot roast mac and cheese, barbecue chicken mac and cheese, plain mac and cheese, hot dogs and chips, fresh pack tomatoes, seasonal cake, and apples and caramel dippers should do the trick.

Pinocchio's Village Haus

DDP: One credit (Q) / Cost: $
TYPE: Italian; Quick Service; Lunch and Dinner

Walk through the castle, pass by the carousel on your right, and on your left adjacent to It's a Small World, you'll find this casual, Italian counter with tables and umbrellas out front. If you're a fan of flatbreads, chicken Parmesan, chicken Alfredo, or Caesar salad with chicken, this is your kind of place. Mickey Check meals are available, the usual kid favorites, and gelato, yogurt, or a chocolate chip cookie for desert.

Be Our Guest

DDP: One credit (T) / Cost: $-$$ (TiW for dinner only)
TYPE: French; Unique/Themed; Breakfast, Lunch, and Dinner

If you've spoken to friends who've recently visited Walt Disney World, you've probably heard about how difficult it is to nab a reservation at this extremely popular, surprisingly elegant, deliciously inventive French restaurant. Start six months in advance if you want a hard-to-get reservation here. Find it at the base of the Beast's castle in the very back of Fantasyland.

Breakfast and lunch are "casual." Dinner is "special and unique." There are three dining rooms: the dark and brooding medieval West Wing with the famous rose under glass; the light, airy, and sumptuous Ballroom complete with chandeliers and views of softly falling snow through the windows; and the sweet Rose Gallery (only used for lunch) with twirling figures of Belle and the Beast. American appetites can easily find something wonderful, but the French touch is just as enticing.

Breakfast is hearty enough to please even Gaston. Eggs and bacon, veggie quiche, croque madame, meats and cheese with a toasted baguette all come sided with fresh fruit. Look for heavenly croissant donuts on the menu.

Lunch features the yummy croque monsieur sandwich, along with carved turkey and roast beef sandwiches, braised pork, tuna salad niçoise, quinoa salad, and veggie quiche. Desserts are a hard-to-choose-from variety of specialty cupcakes and French pastries.

Dinner is lavish. Start with charcuterie, French onion soup, Marseilles mussels, or potato leek soup. Select from among beef, pork, chicken, lamb, and fish entrées, and a vegetable ratatouille. Gourmet cupcakes and French pastries are presented for dessert. You can even "try the grey stuff—it's delicious." It's also a chocolate shell filled with cookie créme.

Drinks here are just as special as the menu. Non-alcoholic beverages in souvenir light-up cups are appealing for kids. An impressive list of fine wines from California and France pairs well with the menu. European breweries are well represented.

You'll find it hard to go wrong at Be Our Guest—providing you can get a table. Everyone wants to eat here!

Cinderella's Royal Table

DDP: Two credits / Cost: $$$-$$$$ (TiW)
TYPE: American; Character; Fine/Signature; Breakfast, Lunch, Dinner

Cinderella Castle has always been the iconic symbol for Walt Disney World, and not only is it one of the best scenic backdrops in the park, you'll have the chance to see it from the inside if you book a character meal here during your stay—but it'll cost you two credits (though you won't have to leave a tip, as an 18% gratuity is included).

It's hard *not* to feel like royalty in this restaurant. As you enter, you'll have the opportunity to be photographed with Cinderella herself against a lavish background. The dining room resembles a medieval banquet hall complete with soaring ceilings, bright banners, and stained glass windows. The Fairy Godmother plays hostess, while some combination of Cinderella, Snow White, Ariel, Jasmine, Sleeping Beauty, and/or Belle drop by your table for a chat. Let's face it, you're not here for the food as much as you are for the experience of dining in the castle and meeting the princesses.

Don't expect to linger. Courses come back-to-back. Still, you can find just about whatever your royal heart desires on the menu...including Dom Pérignon champagne for $320! Breakfast is traditional with inventive options such as beef tenderloin and egg, shrimp and grits or caramel apple stuffed French toast. You'll find healthy choices and vegetarian entrées at each meal. Mickey Check meals are available, naturally, but so are kid-friendly indulgences. Lunch and dinner menus are the same: pork, beef, chicken, fish, vegetable couscous, each prepared in a way sure to please the most demanding princess. Chocolate mousse or sometimes flourless chocolate cake, sugar-free lemon sorbet, carrot-pineapple cake (billed as Bruno-the-Horse's favorite), and Cinderella's s'mores for the kids are sure to finish your regal dining experience to perfection. Don't miss this one!

Tomorrowland

When Disneyland opened in 1955, Walt Disney had this to say about Tomorrowland:

> A vista into a world of wondrous ideas, signifying Man's achievements. A step into the future, with predictions of constructed things to come. Tomorrow offers new frontiers in science, adventure and ideals. The Atomic Age...the challenge of Outer Space...and the hope for a peaceful, unified world.

By the time Tomorrowland opened at Walt Disney World in 1971 with only two attractions up and running, the company rethought the concept a bit. The future has a habit of catching up with the present, so a retro kind of Jules Verne-inspired theme, it was hoped, wouldn't seem so quickly dated.

You'll find large counter-service dining choices here. Snack options abound, but don't expect to teleport into any fancy restaurants or character meals. It's all casual and quick.

Tomorrowland Kiosks, Wagons, and Carts

Cool Ship Cooling Station has a constantly rotating menu, but cool drinks are always available, usually with Mickey pretzels and occasionally corn dogs, too.

Only on busy days, Space Dogs near the PeopleMover sells hot dogs, and a cart selling turkey legs may be found during busy times near the Astro Orbiter.

A newcomer to Tomorrowland is Joffrey's Revive where you can wake yourself up with a wide variety of coffee and tea— plain or fancy. There's a Dreamsicle Iced Latte, Dulce de Leche Iced Latte, and an Island Swizzle Iced Tea.

Smell popcorn on the breeze? Yes, a popcorn cart is located in Tomorrowland, too, and it's right beside an ice cream cart.

Auntie Gravity's Galactic Goodies

DDP: No / Cost: $
TYPE: American;. Quick service; Snacks and Breakfast

Journey past Cosmic Ray's and you'll come to Auntie Gravity's on the same side of the walkway. It forms a triangle with Cool Ship and the popcorn and ice cream carts near the entrance to Space Mountain. This is the perfect spot for a quick, grab-and-go breakfast or a mid-day snack. Muffins, whole pieces of fruit, assorted cereals and milk, and fruit smoothies will pair well with coffee, hot or iced, and cocoa. Vanilla, chocolate, or swirl ice cream can be put into a float, cup, cone, or sundae.

Cosmic Ray's Starlight Café

DDP: One credit (Q) / Cost: $
TYPE: American; Quick Service; Lunch and Dinner

Walking past the Mad Tea Party teacups through the "back door" into Tomorrowland, the first quick-service dining place you'll see is this modern, counter service restaurant, on your right. It's great for a casual meal. All three "bays" now offer the same menu items: barbecued pork sandwich, barbecued pork/bacon cheeseburger, grilled chicken sandwich, chicken nuggets,

Greek salad with chicken, falafel burger or half a rotisserie chicken with mashed potatoes and green beans. Sides are fries, green beans, and cheese dip. You'll find Mickey Check meals and many kid-appealing entrées. The toppings bar surprises with add-ons like sautéed mushrooms and onions, grilled onions, sriracha, aioli, and jalapeños. Ray's has desserts, too, such as triple-chocolate cake, s'mores, and yogurt.

The Lunching Pad

DDP: One credit (Q) / Cost: $
TYPE: American; Quick Service; Lunch and Dinner

Walk 180 degrees around the Astro Orbiter and People-Mover. On the opposite side facing toward the central hub, you'll find this name-tells-all counter—although it could just as well be called the Dining Pad, but *that* wouldn't be a pun. All-beef hot dogs come with apple slices or chips, and there are ham and cheese-stuffed pretzels or cream cheese pretzels on the menu. Frozen carbonated beverages come with souvenir Mickey straws. Orange juice, milk and soy milk, regular or chocolate milk, coffee and tea, and many other beverages (like Fanta!) are sold here.

Tomorrowland Terrace Restaurant

DDP: One credit (Q) / Cost: $
TYPE: American; Quick Service; Lunch and Dinner

Sit on the pretty outdoor terrace overlooking Cinderella Castle for a gorgeous backdrop at your counter-serve lunch or dinner. Tomorrowland Terrace is open seasonally during busy times. A 1/3 pound Angus bacon cheeseburger with apple slices or fries should quell any rumbling stomachs. Slightly lighter fare like a chicken Caesar salad is served, along with selections like chicken strips, a spicy Asian banh mi pulled pork sandwich, and a smoked sausage sandwich. Coconut tres leches cake, a rocky road brownie, or Greek yogurt can be enjoyed alone or with a meal. Mickey Check meals (Smucker's Uncrustables) are on the menu as well as other entrées kids will enjoy (mac and cheese, chicken strips). There's a great view of Happily Ever After fireworks at night.

You've just taken a culinary tour through the Magic King-dom, starting on Main Street, U.S.A. and heading clockwise around the entire park focusing on the many places to satisfy just about any appetite, from the heartiest to the lightest, the most adventurous to the most selective. You'll also find options here to accommodate every budget. Some of your choices are sit-down fancy affairs like Cinderella's Royal Table, some are delightful character meals/buffets like the Crystal Palace, and some are inventive new dining adventures like Skipper's Canteen. Whether you feel like a quick bite of some-thing satisfying on the run, such as Casey's corn dog nuggets, or you're eating healthy and looking for fresh fruit, Greek yogurt, or perhaps that famous pineapple Dole Whip treat, you're sure to find it at the Magic Kingdom.

Next, let's take a stroll through Epcot, the park many guests consider to be the Holy Grail of Walt Disney World dining expe-riences. As Julia Child frequently encouraged, "Bon appétit," and you're going to *need* a good appetite while visiting Epcot!

Epcot, Part One
Future World, United Kingdom, Canada, France, Morocco, and American Adventure

Epcot is, without a doubt, the theme park with the most appealing, international selection of good things to eat. The park opened in 1982, eleven years after the Magic Kingdom. With eleven pavilions from as many nations, it's like a mini-around-the-world vacation extravaganza. One thing you'll notice is that this park is divided into two distinct halves, a Future World and a sort of permanent World's Fair called the World Showcase. In this chapter, we'll cover all of Future World as well as the pavilions of Canada, the United Kingdom, France, Morocco, Japan, and the American Adventure.

Originally, Walt Disney envisioned his grand plan in the Florida countryside as a social experiment he called the Experimental Prototype Community of Tomorrow, EPCOT for short. That's right, the word was spelled in all capital letters back when it was an acronym. It was to have been a place where people would live, work, and play together in security and harmony. Public transportation would be plentiful and would feature PeopleMovers and monorails. The self-contained community would show the rest of the world how life should be lived. There wasn't even a theme park in the original plans for Walt Disney World at all, let alone four of them. Investors refused to sign on, however, without a "draw," something like the hugely popular Disneyland in Anaheim. Thus, the Magic Kingdom was created. Walt passed away in 1966, five years before the grand opening of Walt Disney World, and never saw his Florida plan realized. Still, his dream is the one responsible for its creation.

At this point, the "living, working, and playing" concept has largely been set aside in favor of a recreation destination where families can come for vacations without ever needing to leave the extensive grounds, all 27,000+ acres of them. Epcot is large, too. The Magic Kingdom is about 100 acres inside the park perimeter, while Epcot is more like 300 acres—and we'll cover them all in this guide. Don't be surprised if you need *lots* of refueling stops!

Future World

The giant, silver sphere known as Spaceship Earth anchors the first "land" of Epcot and is the representative symbol of the park itself. All things fast-paced and streamlined will be found here, from amusement park rides you can design and try out for yourself, to a working test track for cars of the future. Everything looks ahead, and the emphasis is on technology. The Seas and The Land are two large areas contained within Future World, both of them providing guests with appealing choices for meals.

Future World Kiosks, Carts, and Wagons

Before you even enter the park, you'll see a little stand next to the monorail entrance called Coffee-Espresso-Pastries, and that's just what you'll find being served there. In the fall, they serve hot or iced pumpkin pie latte and warm, apple-spiced harvest latte topped with whipped cream. During warmer times of the year, grab a refreshing peach iced tea or iced coffee.

The Test Track Cool Wash station is a small kiosk near the busy Test Track. When it's open during very busy times, you'll find slushes, drinks, and *sometimes* snacks.

Popcorn carts move around, but if you find one, it might offer some unusual, savory, gourmet flavors. A turkey leg cart is sometimes open when the park is very busy.

The Land Cart near The Land Pavilion offers fresh fruit and cheeses, Mickey pretzels with dipping cheese, a veggie plate, hummus and pretzels, and lots of beverages including beers.

Taste Track

DDP: One credit (S) / Cost: $
TYPE: American; Quick Service; Snacks

This little snack venue located near the entrance to Test Track has ice cream treats, from sundaes and floats to ice cream cookie sandwiches and waffle cones. It's open seasonally.

Electric Umbrella

DDP: One credit (Q) / Cost: $
TYPE: American; Quick Service; Lunch and Dinner

On the left side of the fountain, as you're walking into the park past Spaceship Earth, you'll find a counter restaurant for lunch or dinner. There is seating inside, so rest your feet and dig into some burgers, chicken nuggets, a chicken breast salad, veggie "naan"wich, sausage and pepper sandwich, or vegetarian flatbread. A chilled chicken wrap is the Mickey Check meal, but kids can order many of the above choices plus the ever-popular mac and cheese. Finish up with a chocolate cupcake, a mixed fruit cup, a sugarless brownie, or strawberry cheesecake.

Fountain View

DDP: One credit (Q) / Cost: $
TYPE: American; Quick Service; Snacks and Breakfast

For a pick-me-up shot of espresso or a tall, cool frappuccino, look for the big fountain just past the silver dome of Spaceship Earth. Fountain View will be to the right as you walk toward the World Showcase. Customizable coffee, crème (no coffee), smoothies, teas, refreshers, hot cocoa, and all your favorite Starbucks signature beverages like white chocolate mocha or caramel macchiato are found right here. You can grab a wake-me-up beverage and nice assortment of breakfast sandwiches on your way in or a "Midnight Mint" or "S'mores" frappuccino on your way out.

Sunshine Seasons

DDP: One credit (Q) / Cost: $
TYPE: Global; Quick Service; Breakfast, Lunch, and Dinner

This restaurant is virtually all things to all guests, boasting a wide variety of fresh and tasty items on its menu. Find it in

The Land Pavilion, which will be on your right as you move toward the World Showcase. Once you're there, first, get a table. Sometimes they're in short supply. Then, walk through the length of the restaurant so as not to miss any of the counters.

Each counter has its own specialties: Asian Noodles (Mongolian beef, shrimp stir fry, vegan korma, sweet and sour chicken with jasmine rice), Soups (pumpkin, roasted tomato, chicken corn chowder) and Salads (seared tuna with Asian noodle, Caesar, and a power salad), Sandwiches (fish tacos and veggie flatbread, too), the Grill (salmon, pork chop, chicken), and a Kid's Zone that seems to have something for just about every child (Smucker's Uncrustables, spaghetti with turkey meatballs, salmon, panini, chicken drumstick, grilled cheese). All kinds of beverages and desserts, both sinful and healthful, can be found in the grab-and-go stations.

This is a great place to take a break and relax while satisfying food preferences for every member of your party.

Coral Reef Restaurant

DDP: One credit (T) / Cost: $$ (TiW))
TYPE: Seafood/American; Unique/Themed; Lunch and Dinner

As you walk through the main entrance to Epcot, you will come to The Seas on your right. The Coral Reef is next to the Nemo & Friends attraction. It sometimes offers dining events; check in advance of your trip to see what might be available during your visit. In August 2017, Coral Reef went through a much-needed refurbishment.

Lunch and dinner here are termed unique/themed dining experiences, and they certainly are. One request well worth making is to ask for a seat near the enormous circular saltwater aquarium, the biggest one in the world. At more than 200 feet across, it's home to more than 4,000 sea creatures. The 165 feet in diameter Spaceship Earth could be *fully immersed* in the aquarium without touching the sides!

The specialty food here, naturally, is seafood, but you'll find many other items on the menu as well. The entire experience feels like you're dining underwater; from the ceiling to the lamps to the carpeting, everything adds to the illusion. There is no difference in price between the lunch and dinner menus.

This is the newest trend throughout Walt Disney World—hoping to save money at lunch isn't a valid strategy these days.

Start with the restaurant's signature lobster bisque, satiny smooth with a touch of brandy. Entrées include pork, chicken, steak, mahi mahi, shrimp and grits, and salmon, along with a "vegetarian chicken breast" and vegetables. Desserts are inventive. Try a chocolate wave with raspberry gelato, the coconut mango chiffon cake, or a Baileys and Jack Daniels mousse with a caramel crisp. Mickey Check meals are whole pasta or grilled chicken tenders.

The illusion of dining "under the sea" makes this restaurant a popular choice.

Garden Grill
DDP: One credit (T) / Cost: $$-$$$ (TiW)
TYPE: American; Character Buffet; Breakfast, Lunch and Dinner

In The Land Pavilion, one level above Soarin' and Sunshine Seasons, is the charming Garden Grill, a family-style restaurant where tables are visited by costumed characters, usually Chip 'n Dale and sometimes Mickey and/or Pluto. There are occasionally dining events, so ask about them in advance of your vacation. The restaurant rotates slowly to give everyone a view of four different themes (desert, prairie, rainforest, and farmhouse) throughout the course of the meal.

Cuisine is American with some of the offerings grown on-site in the Living with the Land greenhouses. It's an all-you-care-to-enjoy, hearty harvest meal. For breakfast, expect the usual filling fare of bacon or ham and eggs, Mickey waffles, Chip's sticky bun bake, fruit, and biscuits with gravy. Lunch and dinner include warm bread, beef, turkey, Italian sausage and peppers, sweet potato fries, mashed potatoes, mac and cheese, garden veggies, herbed stuffing, and is topped off with a fresh berry shortcake.

World Showcase Promenade
Eleven pavilions representing Canada, the United Kingdom, France, Morocco, Japan, the United States, Germany, Italy, China, Norway, and Mexico ring a scenic, 46-acre lagoon.

There are step-saving tips like taking one of the two ferry boats across the lake, but if you are like most of us, you'll want to see something of every country. That means walking—and *plenty* of it. This theme park is so large that it makes sense to visit Epcot over two days if you possibly can.

Promenade Refreshments

DDP: One credit (Q) / Cost: $
TYPE: American; Quick Service; Snacks, Lunch, and Dinner

For a casual snack or quick meal, stop here before getting started on your trip around the Showcase—but remember, there are many international delights just waiting to be sampled just a few steps ahead. Find hot dogs or chili dogs with ranch kettle chips, beverages including several beers, and fountain drinks here. There is also soft-serve orange, vanilla, and swirl.

Refreshment Port

DDP: One credit (Q) / Cost: $
TYPE: American; Quick Service; Snacks, Lunch, and Dinner

Not to interject myself into your party's private discussion, but if you're talking snack options at this point, please allow me to *highly* recommend the warm croissant donuts (known elsewhere as cronuts) at the Refreshment Port. Sugar and spice and everything nice—including soft serve on top, if you so desire—makes this stop a definite *yes*! Are you feeling exceptionally throw-calorie-counting-to-the-wind? Then try the hot cocoa with Godiva liqueur. Chicken nuggets and fries are on the menu, too. But don't pass up the cronuts; you won't find them just anywhere.

Canada Pavilion

Canada Kiosks, Wagons, and Carts

Keep an eye out for a cart called Popcorn in Canada. It carries Le Fin du Monde, Moosehead, and Lebatt draft beers, available with souvenir mugs, as well as chilled maple café and Crown Royal maple whiskey. Maple is the order of the day in Canada, as you'll soon see.

Le Cellier Steakhouse

DDP: Two credits (T) / Cost: $$$ (TiW)
TYPE: Canadian; Fine/Signature; Lunch and Dinner

Le Cellier recently joined the Disney Dining Plan, and because of the expensive menu selections, it will cost you *two* dining plan credits. Reservations are hard to come by. Six months before your vacation is not too soon to make yours. Le Cellier is intended to be just what it sounds like, the romantic wine cellar of a lovely Canadian château.

For starters, guests rave about the cheddar soup made with Moosehead beer and Nueske's applewood-smoked bacon or baked triple-cream Brie with marmalade, baby greens, and hazelnut praline. There are heirloom tomatoes, charcuterie, and a variety of cheeses, as well. Entrées are both satisfying and beautifully prepared. Filet mignon, poulet rouge, root vegetable gnocchi, Angus NY strip steak, pan-roasted wild king salmon, and Angus rib-eye make for choices to delight the most reticent palate. For a serious splurge, calorie and wallet-wise, try the sublime Porterhouse steak for two. It comes with lobster mac-and-cheese, loaded mashed potatoes, crispy onions, a perfect Bérnaise sauce, and blue cheese fondue—all for the rather princely sum of $119. Not on the dining plan but tempting nonetheless (these are out-of-pocket expenses) are specialty soups and sides such as truffle fries, French onion soup, seared Hokkaido scallops, and an authentic Montreal poutine with Gruyère, smoked brisket, and French onion gravy.

If you have room left for dessert, you won't be disappointed. Maple sugar pecan donuts with whiskey caramel and coffee mousse, nanaimo pie (trust me on this one—chocolate hazelnut crust, coconut custard, and crème anglaise), sometimes maple crème brûlée, blueberry cheesecake, and some fruity, sugar-free delights remain to be savored at your leisure.

For children already cultivating a sophisticated palate, Mickey Check meals are grilled chicken and seared salmon. Steak, mac and cheese, chicken, pasta, and a decadent chocolate mousse will hit just the right notes for children.

Le Cellier is justifiably celebrated for its superlative wine list, and you'll receive expert advice on pairings. The regions of Côtes du Rhône, Saint Estephe, and Chablis, France, plus Napa,

California, provide the wine. You may be tempted by the ice wine flight: Meeker Frozen, Inniskillen Vidal, and Neige Apple.

United Kingdom Pavilion

United Kingdom Kiosks Wagons, and Carts

The seasonal UK Beer Cart serves a variety of British draft beers and ales in souvenir cups. Pear cider is on the menu. Pair a drink with house-made, seasoned, potato crisps—*we* call those "chips" on this side of the pond.

Yorkshire County Fish Shop

DDP: One credit (Q) / Cost: $
TYPE: British; Quick Service; Snacks, Lunch, and Dinner

This picturesque counter restaurant serves up that old British (and American!) favorite: fish and chips. Piping hot and crispy fresh, it's a real winner. Also try real Victorian sponge cake with jam and buttercream or a piece of whole fruit. Fountain beverages are available, and so is Bass Ale or Harp Lager Draft.

Rose and Crown Pub

DDP: No / Cost: $
TYPE: British; Unique/Themed; Snacks, Lunch, and Dinner

Casual, Cockney, and cozy, this pub welcomes you to sit a spell and enjoy a snack or meal and a drink. Table service is available. Traditional British pub grub is exactly what you'll find here: battered banger and chips (sausage and chips, or fries as we call them), fish and chips, and Scotch egg (hard boiled egg wrapped in sausage and deep-fried). The drink menu is filled with lagers, stouts, ales, wines and sangria, pub blends, Scotch whiskey and whiskey flights, port, cognac, and house specialties like the Welsh Dragon, the Leaping Leprechaun, and the Cider and Fireball. Lift a glass, and lift your spirits!

Rose and Crown Dining Room

DDP: One credit (T) / Cost: $$ (TiW)
TYPE: British; Unique/Themed; Lunch and Dinner

For relaxed dining, take a break either inside or on the outdoor patio (which is great for watching IllumiNations at night).

Fare is traditional British. For starters, try the Coronation Salad, St. James smoked salmon, potato-leek soup, house-made meat pie, Scotch egg, or UK cheese platter. Main courses are crowd-pleasers. Go British, but everyone should be able to find something appealing. Fish and chips, bangers and mash, Welsh pub burger, shepherd's pie, vegetable cottage pie, corned beef and cabbage, Scottish salmon, and chicken masala curry are among the many UK favorites, but there are steaks, too. Ever long to try Yorkshire pudding, mushy peas (surprisingly tasty), or bubble and squeak (a pan fried vegetable mixture)? Here's your chance. Tarts, cakes, lemon scones, a wonderful "sticky toffee pudding," and English trifles are the sweet treats.

Flights of Scotch are available, along with many other beverages for both kids and adults. Be sure to check out the "pub blends," which are half one thing and half another, like bass ale and Guinness, cider and Guinness, and plenty more.

France Pavilion

France Kiosks, Wagons, and Carts

Crepes des Chefs de France is a charming kiosk featuring oh-so-sweet crepes with Nutella (Europe's favorite taste sensation), lemon, strawberry, or sugar. To gild the lily, you can put ice cream on top! Add an espresso, a cappuccino, or even a Kronenbourg 1664, a beer brewed in Alsace, France.

Le Vins des Chefs de France, open seasonally, is your chance to sample Chardonnay, Vouvray, Cabernet, Merlot, Beaujolais, and other regional French wines. Non-alcoholic beverages are also available.

L'Artisan des Glaces

DDP: One credit (S) / Cost: $)
TYPE: French; Quick Service; Snacks

Head to the back of the France Pavilion and look for a picturesque tower. Therein, find all manner of ice cream and sorbet to tempt and delight the palate. Try an ice cream martini for something unique and strictly for adults, or make the kids happy with a chocolate macaron ice cream sandwich. Flavors change seasonally, but there are always plenty of them from which to choose. Cool weather specialties include cinnamon with carmelized pecan; cinnamon, caramelized apple and crumble crunch; or candied peanuts with chocolate peanut butter fudge coffees, any of which are sure to wake you right up!

Les Halles Boulangerie-Patisserie

DDP: One credit (Q) / Cost: $
TYPE: French; Quick Service; Snacks, Lunch, and Dinner

Want a taste of France but aren't ready for a full, table-service meal at this point in your day? Find tasty foods here that are very different from the usual park fare. French hot and cold sandwiches, salads, croque monsieur, quiche (Lorraine and Florentine), or perhaps a lovely lobster bisque with half a fresh-baked baguette, are sure to satisfy your craving for something fresh and delicious. Save room for a sweet from the extensive selection that includes chocolate croissants, brioche chocolat, palmiers (cinnamon or chocolate elephant ears), beignets, cookies, puff pastries, chocolate mousse, and many, *many* more.

Les Chefs de France

DDP: One credit (T) / Cost: $$ (TiW for lunch only)
TYPE: French; Unique/Themed dining; Lunch and Dinner

When other restaurants are packed, you can sometimes find a table open here. This establishment makes you feel like you've happened upon a French bistro in one of the Parisian *arrondissements*. The menu was created by three famous French chefs: Paul Bocuse, Gaston Lenotre, and Roger Vergé. Jerome Bocuse, Paul's son, still manages the Epcot French restaurants today. Look for photos on the wall of the original chefs.

Nouvelle cuisine changes seasonally, and you may order from either an a la carte or the *prix fixe* menu. If you're not feeling quite adventurous enough to try the *casserole d'escargots* (snails in casserole), perhaps you'll find the satiny *bisque de homard* (lobster bisque) more to your liking. Charcuterie, a selection of French cheeses, crisp salads, and salmon tartare are some other prelude options. You can't go far wrong with French onion soup. Beef, seafood, duck, flatbreads, and many spectacular vege-tarian plates are available. Naturally, the desserts are sheer perfection. Crème brûlée, chocolate mousse, a strawberries and cream cake with raspberry sauce, a strawberry sorbet, or other assorted sorbets will finish your meal *très bon* in the French style. If you really want to impress, order a Cygne au chocolat and watch eyes pop as you dig into a delicate swan-shaped cream puff filled with chocolate mousse, drizzled with chocolate sauce, and sided with chocolate ice cream. *Mon dieu!*

If you prefer, the three-course *prix fixe* meal allows no substitutions, but there are plenty of appealing choices; it provides the opportunity to try the best of the choices on the menu at this lovely bistro.

Monsieur Paul

DDP: Two credits (T) / Cost: $$$
TYPE: French;. Fine/Signature; Dinner

Just upstairs from Les Chefs de France, you'll find the *très elegante* Monsieur Paul. Again, if you want a full-service dinner and don't have an advance dining reservation, try here, especially if you're willing to dine earlier or later than usual. You can *sometimes* find a table on relatively short notice, especially during the off season, but reservations are recommended.

It bills itself as "gourmet dining" with "inventive twists on traditional French cuisine." The setting is romantic with a wonderful view overlooking the lake, especially from the window seats. There is a "strict dress code":

> Appropriate attire for men includes khakis, slacks, jeans, dress shorts and collared shirts; appropriate attire for women includes capris, skirts, dresses, jeans and dress shorts. Attire that will not be permitted includes tank tops or hats for gentleman, swimwear, cut offs or torn clothing. In addition, while T-shirts are allowed, T-shirts featuring offensive language and/or graphics are not.

There's an indulgent *prix fixe* menu which will set you back *two* dining plan credits *plus* $30.50. The menu features chicken, fish, duck, beef, lamb, and a large selection of appetizers (oxtail soup with truffles, wild caught frog legs, grilled Maine lobster) and desserts (chocolate sphere, Brittany shortbread, or floating islands). A children's menu is also available.

It's a splurge, but the first-rate food makes it an eminently satisfying one!

Morocco Pavilion

Morocco Kiosks, Wagons, and Carts

There is a Spice Road Table Juice Bar counter attached to the restaurant of the same name that serves alcoholic and non-alcoholic slushy drinks, fruit smoothies, and beers. During busy seasons, ice cream (house made) and baklava is sold here as well. If you're looking for juice, however, look elsewhere. They don't have it.

Tangierine Café

DDP: One credit (Q) / Cost: $ ($14.99)
TYPE: Moroccan; Quick Service; Snacks, Lunch, and Dinner

Shawarma is a long skewer of roasting lamb, chicken, or other meat from which slices are cut, and you'll find it at this counter. Get it on a platter sided with hummus, tabouleh, and couscous salad served with fresh Moroccan bread. Chicken, lamb, or falafel wraps come with couscous and lentil salad. There's a kefta (meatball) platter, saffron rotisserie chicken and rice, and a vegetable platter. For kids, hamburgers and chicken nuggets are on the menu. A variety of sides are served. Try a glass of Moroccan wine, sangria, or imported or domestic beer with your meal. Non-alcoholic beverages including a delicious frozen fruit drink are available, too.

Restaurant Marrakesh

DDP: One credit (T) / Cost: $$ (TiW)
TYPE: Moroccan; Unique/Themed; Lunch and Dinner

The smallest of the eleven pavilions, Morocco nevertheless offers you some exciting dining opportunities, especially if you want to try something off the beaten gustatory path. A family-friendly belly dancer (yes, it's possible) entertains on the hour, accompanied by live musicians. Northern Mediterranean foods served in a sultan's palace setting is an escape from the ordinary. And, unlike most other Disney World restaurants nowadays, lunch entrées at Marrakesh are less expensive than those at dinner.

Adventurous appetizers feature thin layers of pastry with fillings such as beef and eggs, seafood, or chicken. There are also soups, salads, and some samplers for two if you'd prefer to try a variety. Entrées with couscous abound. Try it with chicken, lamb, beef, or veggies. Roast lamb, lemon chicken, shish kebobs, and salmon offer choices to please most. Want to try several? Order the Sultan's Sampler. Desserts with pastry and vanilla ice cream or a fruit salad with mint ice cream complete the experience. Don't overlook the long list of specialty drinks, like Casablanca Sunset, Marrakesh Express, and Sahara Splash.

Dining here is a lovely experience and definitely one you won't find around every corner of the bazaar.

Spice Road Table

DDP: One credit (T) / Cost: $$ (TiW)
TYPE: Moroccan; Unique/Themed; Lunch and Dinner

On the lagoon side of the Morocco Pavilion, look for this full-service restaurant with lots of atmosphere. There's a romantic, candlelight dinner available, and you can sit right on the water to watch IllumiNations.

There are so many Mediterranean small plates that it would be hard *not* to find something you'd like to try! Among them are hummus fries, fried calamari, garlic shrimp, rice-stuffed grape leaves, chicken roll, and fresh fish cakes. Three lamb sliders, yellow fin tuna, rack of lamb, vegetable platter, roast chicken, and a mixed grill skewer are among the entrées, with beef sliders and chicken kebobs featured on the children's menu. How about a chocolate pyramid for dessert, saffron and lemon custard, or a selection of baklava? Live a little by trying something from the extensive list of inventive specialty drinks showcasing this region of the world, such as a refreshing pitcher of the house's signature sangria. Moroccan beers and non-alcoholic beverages like Watermelon Delight (watermelon and cranberry juice with orange water) are also available.

Remember to request a table by the water—you'll be glad you did.

Japan Pavilion

Japan Kiosks, Wagons, and Carts

Kabuki Café is a handy place to sample Japanese snacks like miso soup, edamame, sushi, and kakigōri (refreshing shaved ice, flavored and sweetened). Offerings vary with the seasons.

Hot or cold sake is available at the Japan Beverage Stand, and there's also a sake bar found *inside* the Mitsukoshi Department Store.

Katsura Grill

DDP: One credit (Q) / Cost: $
TYPE: Japanese; Quick Service; Snacks, Lunch, and Dinner

Maybe you're not quite ready to jump into the deep-end of Japanese dining. In that case, this little counter may be precisely right for you. Everything is very reasonably priced and the choices are many. Take the stairway up to the counter and find tables, covered or out in the fresh air. Sushi, noodles (both ramen and udon), garlic shrimp, chicken and beef teriyaki, chicken cutlet curry, and other selections will give you a taste of the Orient without being more than you bargained for. Rice, edamame, and miso soup are side orders. Desserts may include green tea cheesecake, green tea ice cream, and azuki (red bean) strawberry ice cream. Kids' versions of most of the entrées are on the menu. Hot or cold sake, plum wine, and a variety of Japanese beers, specialty drinks, and non-alcoholic beverages are available to accompany your meal.

Teppan Edo

DDP: One credit (T) / Cost: $$ (TiW)
TYPE: Japanese; Unique/Themed; Lunch and Dinner

Climb the wide flight of stairs outside and ascend to the Far East. Teppan-style dining means your chefs will prepare your meal from a center grill while you watch, and diners have the opportunity to speak directly with those preparing the food. It's an interactive experience, so be prepared for that.

Appetizers are authentically prepared Japanese-style ribs, tempura, edamame, miso soup, and tofu (atsuage style—deep fried). Sushi many ways comes next: volcano roll, spicy salmon tartare roll, shrimp tempura roll, or perhaps you'll opt for a sushi sampler to try several. Entrées will please both Western and Eastern tastes. They are served with salad, rice, udon noodles (thick, wheat flour noodles), and vegetables. Filet mignon, strip steak, julienne beef, salmon, chicken, shrimp, or a seasonal vegetable medley provide guests not only a great meal but an exciting show. Pair your meal with hot or cold sake, beer, or perhaps a sake cocktail. There are plenty of options for children here and non-alcoholic beverages, too.

Some attractive add-on extras are not included with the dining plan. If you want to try grilled lobster, Wagyu steak (fork tender and sublimely succulent), or tuna tataki, be prepared to pay out-of-pocket.

Tokyo Dining
DDP: One credit (T) / Cost: $$ (TiW)
TYPE: Japanese; Unique/Themed; Lunch and Dinner

You'll feel like you've stepped into a serene downtown Tokyo dining establishment. Attention to detail is impeccable. Even the napkins are folded to look like origami art! Ask for a window table and you'll have a perfect view to watch IllumiNations.

Starters like edamame, ramen noodles with shrimp, grilled shrimp salad, and calamari tempura set the tone for a traditional Japanese meal. Lunch and dinner menus and prices are almost identical, with lunch having slightly fewer items on the menu, but both meals have many choices to fit most people's preferences. Steak or chicken, tempura or sushi rolls, nigiri sushi, or sashimi (which is raw seafood for the adventurous), and many ways of enjoying them transport you to Tokyo. With colorful names like Firecracker Rolls, Dragon Monster Rolls, Spicy Crunchy Rolls with Volcano and Dynamite Drizzle, you'll want to expand your sushi dining horizons. Conversely, lots of rice and noodle dishes are available for the more conservative diners among your party. Kids also have somewhat tamer choices such as a teriyaki burger, tempura nuggets, a California roll, or a Kurobuta sausage dog (made from the famed Berkshire black hogs). Green tea and ginger mousse cake are the dessert offerings, along with soft-serve ice cream.

American Adventure Pavilion

American Adventure Kiosks, Wagons, and Carts

Feeling parched and longing to wet your whistle? "Purveyors of Fine American Ale" at Block & Hans will do the job. They serve a variety of American craft brews. Anyone up for a Killer Whale Cream Ale? Pair it with a Mickey pretzel and cheese sauce, take a seat, and watch the world go by.

The Fife and Drum stand has enough on hand for a filling refreshment stop: turkey legs, waffle ice cream cones, the American Dream (a red, white, and blue slushy drink), and popcorn. You'll also find root beer floats, hard orange soda, and a long list of beers, wines, and non-alcoholic beverages.

The name says it all at the All-American Funnel Cake Stand. Get one plain or make it fancy with soft-serve ice cream, apples, chocolate sauce, or powdered sugar. They've just added a cookies and cream variation. Take home a kit if you want to duplicate this treat once the vacation comes to an end.

Liberty Inn

DDP: One credit (Q) / Cost: $
TYPE: American; Quick Service; Lunch and Dinner

With so many other attractive, international choices, you might want to skip this familiar menu, but if it's exactly what you and the kids are craving, it will hit the spot. Burgers, surf and turf, barbecue pork, chicken salad (red craisins, white chicken, and bleu cheese), nuggets, fries, and apple slices are familiar and comfortable for a quick meal or snack. The warm fruit cobbler, mixed fruit cup, or a rocky road mousse brownie will be a sweet end to your meal at the Liberty Inn.

Congratulations, weary world travelers! You have navigated all of Future World and are now past the halfway point in World Showcase. Your dining and snack choices have been abundant and, at least among the pavilions, truly international. If you are dividing your time at Epcot between two (or more) days, enjoy a pleasant night's rest before returning. You've certainly earned it! If not, turn the page because we're forging ahead to some of the very best eating places in all of Walt Disney World.

Epcot, Part Two
Italy, China, Germany, Norway, and Mexico

Rounding the halfway point of the World Showcase Lagoon, you'll encounter some of the most appealing and tasty snacks available on Disney property, as well as some of the best restaurants Disney World has to offer. The central body of water, besides being 47 acres in surface area, requires a full 1.2 mile perimeter walk to completely circle it on foot—and that doesn't count your side trips through the eleven pavilions. That's why you need to take the substantial distances you'll cover into account when planning rest and refreshment stops, particularly if there are small children or seniors in your party.

This second half of the World Showcase contains the pavilions of Italy, Germany, China, Norway, and Mexico. Ready? Let's go!

Italy

Italy Kiosks, Wagons, and Carts
If it's time to refresh the troops, find something cool and sweet from the Gelato Stand in a cup, cone, or waffle bowl. Flavors change frequently. There is usually a standard ice cream cart open seasonally if you'd prefer a Mickey ice cream bar or sandwich, a frozen banana, or an orange cream-sicle bar.

Via Napoli has a pizza window if you don't have time to sit down and savor a meal right now. Otherwise, try Via Napoli itself. Most folks agree that it's the best pizza at Walt Disney World.

Tutto Gusto Wine Cellar

DDP: No / Cost: $
TYPE: Italian; Lounge; Snacks, Lunch, and Dinner

There's more than simply wine in this celler. Think of it as an Italian wine cellar with meats and cheeses. Order "plates for two or more" with cuisines representing the many distinct regions of Italy. Something familiar like meatball sliders, ravioli, or panini might be what you're looking for. Want to branch out from the usual Italian fare? Insulata di mare with lemon shrimp, squid, and octopus is available for the more adventurous. You won't go wrong with Gusto specialties like meatballs Parmigiana, meatball sliders, ziti, or arancini (shrimp- and lobster-fried risotto balls). Cannoli, strawberries and marscapone, tiramisù, chocolate Nutella cake, and other desserts complete the bill of fare.

Tutto Italia Ristorante

DDP: One credit (T) / Cost: $$$ (TiW)
TYPE: Italian; Unique/Themed; Lunch and Dinner

Dine in Old World charm under the glow of chandeliers and surrounded by murals of ancient Rome. You will find the lunch menu less extensive *and* less expensive than dinner, but you'll enjoy wonderful Italian food no matter when you arrive.

The grande antipasto misto is a great way to share samples of many of the appetizers with a dining partner. There are about ten other tempting choices for appetizers. For lunch, choose from Italian salads, pasta, paninis, and beef and fish main courses. The star at lunch is definitely the scaloppine di pollo con funghi e tortellini alla panna; that's chicken breast cutlets, mushrooms, and cheese tortellini in cream sauce, and it's *meravigliosa!* Dinner has much of the same with some additions and higher prices. Risotto with shrimp, fettuccine with campagnoli (hot and spicy Italian sausage), polenta vasugana (polento with braised short ribs), cremagliera d'agnello (sage crusted rack of lamb), as well as inventive beef, fish, and chicken entrées are plentiful. Tutto offers diners eight different interpretations of popular pasta dishes. Desserts include tiramisù, sorbetti e gelati, panna cotta, a lemon ricotta cheesecake with marinated strawberries, cannoli, and a warm hazelnut chocolate cake with vanilla gelato and chocolate sauce. Kids should have no problem with the choice of mozzarella sticks, spaghetti, chicken tenders, and cheese or pepperoni pizza on their menu.

Via Napoli Ristoranti e Pizzeria
DDP: One credit (T) / Cost: $$-$$$ (TiW)
TYPE: Italian; Unique/Themed; Lunch and Dinner

The consensus is that this is where you'll find the best pizza in all of Walt Disney World. It's true, but you'll find plenty of other Italian favorites here, as well. Head to the back of the Italy Pavilion to find Via Napoli. Nick Valenti is in charge of sending to your table the best of what southern Italy has to offer.

Mozzarella caprese (tomato and fresh mozzarella salad) or prosciutto and melon are sure-fire hits to start your culinary tour. Food is baked in three ovens—with *names*! Your dinner will be cooked in Stromboli, Etna, or Vesuvius, each taking its name from a famous volcano of the region. They even have faces, and you can see the fire flickering in their open mouths. Colorful travel posters of Italy line the walls. Many kinds of fresh pasta, parmigiana to please just about everyone in your party, chicken and Caesar salads, and pizzas made fresh to order will leave your group happy with appetites well-satisfied. The mezzo-metro pizza is half a meter (more than 19.6 inches) across! The range of toppings is incredible—just about anything you want on a pizza, you can have on it here. You will find signature specialty pizzas like a white pizza with smoked salmon, a four cheese, a broccolini full of veggies, a spicy picante, and other inventive pies. Four kinds of Italian beer, wine and sangria by the glass, and specialty drinks like Sicilian Sunset, Via Vesuvius, or a Tiramisù Martini are on hand to accompany your meal. There are plenty of non-alcoholic beverages, too.

Germany

Germany Kiosks, Wagons, and Carts
Check out the little bar in the back of Weinkeller, adjacent to the Biergarten, for a variety of German wines. You can get cheeses to pair with them.

The Germany Hövels stand and Germany Bier stand both offer a variety of beers from the different regions of Germany, and Hövels sells pretzels as well. Anyone in the gang game to try Lebkuchenherz beer? It's flavored to taste like gingerbread. How about Schofferhofer (grapefruit beer)?

Karamel-Kuche

DDP: One credit (S) / Cost: $
TYPE: German/American; Quick service; Snacks

This quaint little establishment will remind you of the picturesque caramel shops you've seen in the Werther's Originals advertisements, and sure enough, Werther's is the sponsor. Caramel presented in a virtually endless array of preparations is the order of the day. You'll find tempting caramel apples, caramel popcorn, caramel dipped chocolates and strawberries (and pineapple and grapes, too), caramel marshmallows, caramel pretzels, and more hand-crafted caramel treats than you've ever imagined, made right here in this sweet-smelling caramel kitchen. As many ways and combinations as you can imagine caramel creations being concocted, this shop has *more*! It will be difficult for children (or adults, for that matter) to choose among them, so you might want to pick up a few items while you're here to take home or enjoy later back at your hotel room.

Sommerfest

DDP: One credit (Q) / Cost: $
TYPE: German; Quick Service; Snacks, Lunch, and Dinner

A quick stop at Sommerfest's counter will have you feeling like you've just dropped in on a casual, Bavarian café for the afternoon or evening. Brightly painted Alpine motifs decorate the buildings that surround you. Tables outside let you enjoy German music coming from the nearby Biergarten while munching on reasonably priced brats, frankfurters, nudel gratin (baked mac and cheese with a custard-like texture), and cold potato salad with eggs. The restaurant also specializes in authentic, hand-twisted pretzels. Finish in German style with the deliciously rich Black Forest cake or Bavarian apple strudel. A selection of German beers, bourbon shots, and Riesling wine are available, as well as plenty of non-alcoholic drinks.

Biergarten

DDP: One credit (T) / Cost: $$-$$$
TYPE: German; Unique/Themed; Lunch and Dinner

It's *always* October here at the Biergarten! Next to Sommer-fest and billing itself as a "boisterous buffet," you'll serve your-self up heaping helpings of hearty German food. Octoberfest seating means you will find large, banquet tables where several families are seated together. As you eat, you'll hear lots of rous-ing, lively German folk music. Feel free to clap along or sing if you know the words. The vibe here is rollicking and relaxed.

Cold salads include potato, tomato, cucumber, cabbage, and pasta. They come with pretzel rolls and house-made pickles. Entrées feature pork schnitzel, spätzle (noodles), German meat loaf, sauerbraten, roast pork, beef, platters of sausages, roasted vegetables, and mac and cheese, along with chicken and fish. Apple strudel, cheesecake, chocolate cookies, fruit compote with vanilla sauce, Black Forest cake, and others bring your lavish buffet to a sweet conclusion. You'll find the menu well-stocked with German beers, white wines, red wines, schnapps, and shots. There are, of course, non-alcoholic beverages aplenty.

China

China Kiosks, Wagons, and Carts

The pretty pagoda called the Joy of Tea offers much more than just tea. Have a chicken curry pocket, a barbecue pork bun (heavenly but seasonal), a pork and vegetable egg roll— or sample all three by ordering the Lucky Combo! Hot and cold assorted teas, lucky red bean ice cream, ginger ice cream, alcoholic beverages featuring plum wine, schnapps, gin, and vodka, draft beer, and smoothies or soft drinks will accom-pany that snack nicely.

Lotus Blossom Café

DDP: One credit (Q) / Cost: $
TYPE: Chinese; Quick Service; Snacks, Lunch, and Dinner

If your party wants something fast and delicious, either for a meal or just a snack, walk through the red pillars of the Lotus Blossom. Dine either inside or outside under the eaves.

You'll be delighted with the reasonably priced menu. Maybe the pot stickers and egg rolls are exactly what you need to keep you going. You'll recognize your favorite Chinese take-out items like orange chicken, Mongolian beef noodles, shrimp fried rice, Sichuan spicy chicken, and vegetable stir-fry. Draft beers, plum wine, smoothies, teas, and fountain beverages are served, along with caramel ginger or lychee ice cream.

Nine Dragons Restaurant

DDP: One credit (T) / Cost: $$ (TiW)
TYPE: Chinese; Unique/Themed; Lunch and Dinner

Dine in an elegant setting under the soft glow of Chinese lanterns at Nine Dragons where contemporary Chinese cuisine meets traditional. The price is reasonable and the service is some of the most attentive in the entire park. You'll recognize familiar appetizers like pot stickers, spring rolls, and dumplings, but how about shrimp and taro lollipops? The Chinese steamed buns are exceptionally savory and choices include braised pork and chili aioli, fragrant chicken, General Tsao's chicken, and steamed pork soup dumplings. Whether you'd like to try sweet and sour chicken, sesame chicken, spit-roasted Beijing chicken, barbecue pork, Kung Pao chicken or shrimp, Canton pepper beef, shrimp typhoon, roast duck salad, fragrant five-spiced fish, vegetable tofu, or steak and shrimp, there is a wealth of mouth-watering items from which to choose. Give Shanghai Grandma's red-braised, slow-cooked pork belly a try for a homey taste of old China—it's the chef's choice. An excellent value is the Nine Dragons Family Dinner Set. It includes your choice of soup, entrée, and dessert. Coconut red-rice pudding, Chinese ginger cake, and ice cream are the featured desserts.

Norway

Norway Kiosks, Wagons, and Carts

Stop by the Norway Beer Stand if you need something cool to drink. A glass of wine or beer, fountain beverages and bottled water are sold, as well as Mickey ice cream treats and assorted Lays brand chips.

Kringla Bakeri og Kafe

DDP: One credit (Q) / Cost: $
TYPE: Norwegian;. Quick Service; Snacks, Lunch, and Dinner

This unassuming little café is one of the nicest surprises in all of Epcot. Those in the know never fail to stop here for the justifiably famous bakery treats, accompanied by a good cup of coffee. If you're looking for more than a quick snack but aren't quite ready for a full Norwegian meal at Akershus, try the succulent Norwegian kjøttkake (meatballs), the ham and fresh apple sandwich (sweet apple chutney, Jarlsberg and Muenster cheeses), Norwegian club sandwich, or a smoked salmon and egg sandwich. The Fisherman's Tasting Box is perfect for seafood lovers, and Norwegian charcuterie is another popular pick.

Something this place excels at is pastry—*lots* of pastry. Once you try the Norwegian school bread, you'll be signing up for extra classes! It's a not-overly-sweet cardamom bun filled with vanilla cream custard and coated with toasted coconut. The Viking chocolate mousse is scrumptious and comes with small cookie horns stuck into the sides of a frozen chocolate Viking hat. It's delightful! Chocolate pretzels, the troll horn, rice pudding, and a cinnamon loaf of epic proportions will make everyone in your group want to linger just a little bit longer in Norway, maybe over strong cups of Viking coffee (enhanced with Kamora coffee liqueur and Bailys Irish Cream).

Akershus Royal Banquet Hall

DDP: One credit (T) / Cost: $$$ (TiW)
TYPE: Norwegian; Character Buffet; Breakfast, Lunch, and Dinner

This medieval castle is the perfect place to meet Disney princesses. If you couldn't snag an ADR for Cinderella's Royal Table, Akershus might still have openings. There are no guarantees on exactly which princesses will appear on any given day, but some of the princesses who usually attend are Princess Aurora (Sleeping Beauty), Belle, Ariel, Snow White, and Cinderella.

Breakfast is traditional American fare served family style, but there is also a Norwegian smorgasbord buffet. Lunch and dinner feature Norwegian specialties, so be aware of the menu when planning a visit. The choices are wide enough to please just about everyone. First comes a "Taste of Norway," which includes seafoods, cheeses, fruits, salads, and cured, sliced meats. Next, pan-seared salmon, Norwegian meatballs, grilled pork chop, chicken, beef, a vegan/vegetarian roasted vegetable terrine, and a goat cheese ravioli are the main courses. For dessert, you'll have a choice of Norwegian-inspired treats that make it difficult to try just one. Guests in your party might find themselves sharing bites of the many baked goods. Mickey Check meals feature chicken, salmon, and beef. Macaroni, meatballs, and pizza fill out the children's menu.

If you have breakfast early enough, you may be able to get into line for the new (and hugely popular) Frozen Ever After attraction before a lengthy queue forms. It's worth a try!

Mexico

Mexico Kiosks, Wagons, and Carts
Near the entrance to the World Showcase, which is close to Mexico and next to Disney Traders, you'll find Joffrey's. There are several Joffrey's located in and around Epcot including one between Canada and the UK, one by the Epcot Monorail Station, and one by the American Adventure. You'll see these convenient kiosks throughout the resort, too. Look for giant, pink donuts with sprinkles, lots of bakery goodies, and plenty of coffee and tea choices.

Choza de Margarita
This new kiosk opened in November 2018. In addition to three appealing, hand-crafted margaritas and three frozen margaritas, it also serves "small plates" and quick snacks (tacos on house-made corn tortillas, empanadas, etc.) to grab and go. There's a nice fruit punch, too, which is non-alcoholic.

La Cava del Tequila
DDP: No / Cost: $
TYPE: Mexican; Beverages

Over 200 kinds of tequila are available in this cave of wonders, not to mention some of the best margaritas this side of the border, along with Mexican beers and wines. Chips and salsa or guacamole can accompany your drink selections.

La Cantina de San Angel

DDP: One credit (Q) / Cost: $
TYPE: Mexican; Quick Service; Breakfast, Lunch, and Dinner

This cantina is right on the lagoon overlooking the water. Don't expect to find an American-style breakfast here. The cantina offers breakfast seasonally, while lunch and dinner are served year round. The menu is definitely spicy. Eggs with cheese, chilies, tortillas, and chorizo (Mexican sausage) will certainly wake you up! A milder children's option is available. Lunch and dinner menus are the same, and also feature traditional Mexican food. You can order chicken and rice, tacos (including beef, chicken, or fish tacos), empanadas (here, that means fried flour tortillas filled with cheese), Mexican salad, and nachos. Beans and rice are served with most of the entrées. For kids, cheese empanadas or chicken tenders are available. Desserts are churros (Mexican donuts) and paletas (fruit popsicles). Mexican sodas (called jarritos), Coke products, hot cocoa, and coffee accompany the meals. All that, and you can watch IllumiNations while having dinner—but remember to ask for a table overlooking the water.

La Hacienda de San Angel

DDP: One credit (T) / Cost: $$
TYPE: Mexican; Unique/Themed; Dinner

The dinner menu at La Hacienda is both extensive and inventive. You will find many traditional Mexican favorites, but there are also more exotic offerings to tempt you. Entremeses (appetizers) include a light spinach salad, cream of corn soup with crisp tortilla strips, pork empanadas, gorditas (corn cakes stuffed with Mexican sausage, potatoes, and arugula), and several kinds of fresh cheese sauces, guacamole, and various chili sauces with chips and tortillas. There are interesting plates "for two," one with several varieties of seafood and one with beef and chicken. These come with beans and vegetables. Entrées have enough diversity to please most palates. Steak, chicken, a taco sampler platter, pan-seared snapper, or short ribs with potato purée all come with house-made corn tortillas and rice. Finish the meal with chocolate mousse, fruit sorbet, a caramel apple empanada with dulce de leche ice cream, or the well-known Mexican flan (custard). Service is friendly and attentive, and the flavors are definitely zesty! With grand windows overlooking the lagoon, the view of IllumiNations is simply spectacular.

San Angel Inn Restaurante

DDP: One credit (T) / Cost: $$ (TiW)
TYPE: Mexican; Unique/Themed; Lunch and Dinner

One of the nicest perks of dining at San Angel Inn Restaurante is sitting beside the water indoors in perpetual blue twilight watching the little boats go drifting by, filled with guests on their way to the Gran Fiesta Tour Starring the Three Caballeros. The architecture is modeled in the style of a seventeenth-century hacienda. In the background, a Mayan pyramid is colorfully illuminated. Look for carved stone heads in the Olmec style.

The menu here is like taking a trip to Mexico. In fact, Epcot's version is based on the famous San Angel restaurant in Mexico City. For starters, try the Aztec soup, Acapulco-style shrimp cocktail, chicken tostadas, veggie tacos, or Caesar salad. The main courses aren't your typical Mexican take-out fare. Far from it! You'll find beef, pork, chicken, and fish spiced carefully and sided with sauces and some combination of rice, beans, or vegetables. There are two chef's recommendations that should please hearty appetites. Try the braised short rib, tamale, poblano pepper stuffed with shrimp, queso fresco (fresh cheese), and black beans, or the Veracruz-style catch of the day served over roasted potatoes and a Mexican vegetable medley. Bavarian cream with fresh berries, caramel ice cream, cheesecake with caramel sauce, or chocolate mousse should allow you to savor the ambience here at San Angel before leaving Mexico behind.

It's hard to find a prettier, more romantic spot anywhere at Walt Disney World, and the food is outstanding.

Your head may be spinning and your feet may be protesting by this point in the evening, but your stomach should be very happy. After all, visiting eleven countries is a tall order in just a day or two. Add Future World Epcot to that agenda and you will definitely need a good night's sleep to get rested and ready for more adventures tomorrow. If you thought Epcot was big at 300 acres, just wait. The Animal Kingdom is the second largest theme park in the world, boasting 580 lush acres! Your party can count on finding plenty of good things to eat and drink in order to maintain the stamina to cover such large distances, and those dining options are exactly what you'll find in the next chapter.

Disney's Animal Kingdom, Part One

The Oasis, Discovery Island, Africa, and Rafiki's Planet Watch

Dining choices in the Animal Kingdom are extensive and range from the tame and familiar to the wild and exotic—a lot like the animals you'll encounter here. Those comfortable walking shoes you packed can expect a serious workout today!

The 580-acre Animal Kingdom opened on Earth Day, April 22, 1998, the fourth of the four big Disney theme parks to open in Orlando. It has been expanded and updated several times since then, and more big changes are on the horizon. Coming here is a wonderful way to introduce children to the idea of animal and habitat conservation; education is a big part of the park's mission.

Now that Pandora—the World of Avatar has opened, expect a big uptick in attendance. The new area will add substantial acreage to the already huge Animal Kingdom. You'll see floating islands and bioluminescent plants, and you'll be able to dine at the Satu'li Canteen, a spacious restaurant displaying *objet d'art* from the Na'Vi culture and décor reflecting this gorgeous new world.

Whether you arrive by car or Disney bus, you'll pass a Rainforest Café on the left as you face the entrance gates. It's not inside the park, but because of the restaurant's animal theme, it's a perfect fit for this location. Keep it in mind. You might want to eat here at some point before, after, or even during your visit.

On our "dining safari," we will proceed clockwise and pass through the Oasis, Discovery Island, Africa, Raffiki's Planet Watch, Asia, Pandora, and finally DinoLand U.S.A. If you notice a kaleidoscope of different ideas and kinds of exhibits, you're right. That's because the original concept for Disney's Animal Kingdom, as explained by Michael Eisner at the opening ceremonies back on April 22, 1998, was pretty wide-ranging and ambitious:

> Welcome to a kingdom of animals...real, ancient and imagined: a kingdom ruled by lions, dinosaurs and dragons; a kingdom of balance, harmony and survival; a kingdom we enter to share in the wonder, gaze at the beauty, thrill at the drama, and learn.

To that list, let me add "and *eat*," because you'll undoubtedly be doing a lot of that while you're here.

The Oasis

Rainforest Café
DDP: One credit (T) / Cost: $$
TYPE: American; Unique/Themed; Breakfast, Lunch, and Dinner

The menu here is typically American. What you get, in addition to good food and excellent service, is the ambience of eating in a tropical rainforest filled with animated animals, stars overhead, and even the occasional rainstorm accompanied by lightning and thunder. The bar stools all are painted and designed to resemble the back half of various beasts— zebras, giraffes, tigers, and others. Little ones might find the realism a bit overwhelming, especially the loud sounds of the simulated storm. If you can rouse everyone out of bed early enough (it opens at 8:30 a.m.), you might want to plan a stop at this interesting restaurant before you even pass through the entrance turnstiles to the Animal Kingdom.

Breakfast items are "Jungle Classics" or "Rainforest Favorites," and the kids menu is very appealing. Breakfast includes omelettes (including egg white omelettes), eggs Benedict, French toast, waffles, steak and eggs, oatmeal and fruit, breakfast slider sandwiches, and a hot and spicy Mexican breakfast pizza known as Pie of the Viper. Mimosas, Bloody "Marks," many kinds of specialty coffee drinks, and juices are available.

For lunch and dinner, the menus and prices are the same. Rainforest is known for its large menu with items guaranteed to please just about anyone. Start off with beef lava nachos, crustacean crab dip, or maybe jungle safari soup. Burgers, sandwiches, and fries? Check. Pasta and flatbreads? Check. Soups, salads, seafoods? Check. Beef, chicken, pork? Check and double check! You can even try some reasonably priced add-ons (often referred to nowadays as enhancements) like coconut shrimp, Caribbean rice, red-skinned potatoes, and St. Louis spareribs.

A favorite dessert is the sparkling volcano, built with brownies, vanilla ice cream, whipped cream, and hot fudge and caramel running down the sides. It used to come lit with an actual sparkler, but now the sparkle is a decoration inserted into the top. It's plenty big enough for four to share. If that's too much, then cheesecake, sorbet, a root beer float, or chocolate cake ought to keep the gang happy.

The place is formulaic, but that formula continues to work quite well. The décor and the food are both lots of fun.

Discovery Island

Discovery Island Kiosks, Wagons, and Carts

The Feeding Ground is the clever name for a popcorn wagon on Discovery Island. You can find frozen lemonade for the kids and adult beverages here, too.

The Smiling Crocodile is located on the way to the bridge leading to Asia, just before the Eight Spoon Café on the opposite side of the walkway. Crocodile features three sandwiches—salmon BLT, pimento cheese BLT, or turkey BLT—and you can wash them down with beer or fountain beverages.

Eight Spoon Café is a small walk-up kiosk as you leave Discovery Island and head over the bridge to Asia. Baked mac-and-cheese, either plain or with shrimp and sweet chili sauce or pulled pork, and chips are available, along with fountain beverages and water.

Isle of Java is near the bridge that leads to DinoLand U.S.A. If you want coffee or a morning beverage, Isle has you covered. Pair your drink with muffins, elephant ears, bagels, or a Danish.

Nomad Lounge

DDP: No / Cost: $$
TYPE: African/American; Lounge; Snacks and Drinks

Nomad is next to Tiffins, Discovery Island's signature dining restaurant. If you weren't able to get a table at Tiffins, you can still sample some of the flavors right here, accompanied by a tremendous selection of alcoholic and non-alcoholic beverages. The appetizers are vegetarian pad Thai with spicy peanut sauce, pork ribs,, Asian barbecue chicken wings, charcuterie, a selection of artisanal cheeses, Wagyu beef sliders, and fish tacos. Be sure to try the Tiffin's bread service and maybe churros with vanilla crema or chili-strawberry for dessert. With names like the Tempting Tigress, the Snow Leopard Salvation, or Jenn's Tatoo, choosing a drink will pose quite the challenge!

Terra Treats

DDP: One credit (S) / Cost: $
TYPE: Gluten free/allergy free; Quick Service; Snacks

A little kiosk on the far side of Discovery Island just before the bridge that leads to Africa, Terra Treats is well worth noting. It features snacks for those with food allergies. Selections include hummus and veggies, rice chips, buffalo chicken wings, and sometimes gluten-free bagels and muffins. You can obtain information here about the best places in the park to find non-dairy, sugar-free, gluten-free, and other safe foods.

Creature Comforts

DDP: One credit (Q) / Cost: $
TYPE: American; Quick Service; Snacks

Past Pizzafari on the same side of the walkway, you'll find Creature Comforts—where everything's coming up Starbucks. The long list of hot, cold, and specialty coffee drinks is sure to please anyone looking for a pick-me-up, caffeinated or not. Tea, hot cocoa, milk, or fruit beverages should provide just what you're looking for if coffee isn't your thing. If you'd like to make this a quick breakfast stop or just want a satisfying snack, pick up a Starbucks specialty coffee drink and pair it with a piece of fruit, scone, muffin, danish, croissant, yogurt, pumpkin or banana bread, or iced lemon pound cake. New additions are specialty cupcakes. Try the Tree of Life, Cotton Top Tamarin (a tiny New World monkey), or Zebra for something different—and delicious.

Flame Tree Barbecue

DDP: One credit (Q) / Cost: $ (TiW)
TYPE: American; Quick Service; Lunch and Dinner

Almost directly across from Pizzafari on the opposite side of Discovery Island is Flame Tree Barbecue. Barbecue ribs (if you're ravenous, get the full rack of St. Louis-style ribs) chicken, pulled pork, fruit salad, and smoked turkey are menu favorites here. Sides are fries (with cheese and pulled pork as an add-on; it makes a meal) and onion rings. Mickey Check meals for kids are a chicken sandwich or a Smucker's Uncrustable. Additional kids choices are a baked chicken drumstick or a hot dog. Chocolate or lime mousse is a cool finish to a meal here. There are beers and wines to pair with your food, in addition to lots of non-alcoholic beverages. For the adventuresome imbiber, check out the mandarin orange vodka lemonade; it's guaranteed to beat the heat.

Pizzafari

DDP: One credit (Q) / Cost: $
TYPE: Italian; Quick Service; Snacks, Lunch, and Dinner

As soon as you cross the bridge leading to Discovery Island, Pizzafari will be on your left. Colorful paintings of wild birds and animals in motion enliven the walls of its several dining rooms. A casual atmosphere makes for relaxing dining. Flatbreads like shrimp, Mediterranean, pepperoni, cheese, and cheeseburger are offered, along with salads, pastas, and a meatball sub. Garlic knots and tomato basil soup could make a meal in itself. Mickey Check meals for kids include Mickey pasta with turkey marinara sauce or Smucker's Uncrustables, but kids could opt for cheese pizza or mac and cheese instead. Desserts are chocolate mousse and tiramisù.

Tiffins

DDP: Two credits (T) / Cost: $$$
TYPE: African/Asian/Latin; Fine/Signature; Lunch and Dinner

Directly adjacent to Pizzafari, the popular new Tiffins restaurant is creating a lot of buzz. (Wondering what a "tiffin" is? It means a light lunch, but a lot of the entrées here are hardly in the light category.) Tiffin's is considered to be one of the best places to eat among all the restaurants in the four Disney theme parks. The cuisine mixes African, Asian, and Latin influences, but it is intended to appeal to average American tastes.

Imaginative appetizers include black-eyed pea fritters, seasonal fish causa (Peruvian purple potatoes, lime mayo, aji Amarillo vinaigrette, quail egg), watermelon and barrel-aged feta with toy box tomatoes, marinated and grilled octopus, along with tried-and-true apple-walnut salad, charcuterie, and a selection of Tiffin's signature breads. Favorites like chicken, lamb, pork, halibut, duck, Wagyu strip sirloin,and house-smoked brisket, grilled swordfish, and braised Berkshire pork belly ramen are joined on the list of entrées by whole fried fish and pomegranate-lacquered chicken served with the tiniest of thumbelina carrots, sweet potato, and citrus-fennel salad. Vegetarian curry appears, too. Mickey Check meals for kids are pan-seared fish or grilled chicken, along with kid menu items like grilled beef and pasta marinara.

The desserts are equally exotic: passion fruit tapioca crème and calamansi (citrus-kumquat hybrid) mousse (mango lava, Swiss meringue), among several others, but you'll also be happy with good old chocolate ganache or lime cheesecake. The beverage menu is extensive, with lots of non-alcoholic beverages plus beers and wines from around the world and that same provocatively titled bunch of cocktails served at Nomad Lounge.

The three dining rooms each have a different theme carried out with careful attention to detail. Some have framed drawings used in the early conceptions of the Animal Kingdom. Tiffins is your chance to try something unusual and fabulous!

Africa

Africa Kiosks, Wagons, and Carts

Caravan Road is a kiosk on the pathway between Africa and Asia. When it's open, which is only during busy times of the year, it serves semi-exotic items like teriyaki beef sliders, Asian noodle salad, and edamame.

Dawa Bar, located just outside Tusker's, offers lots of alcoholic drink options, including beer and cleverly concocted cocktails. Dawa sells "Sunrise Cocktails," too, like Tusker Beermosa or Discovery Island Bloody Mary with snow leopard vodka.

Harambe Fruit Market has fresh pineapple spears, strawberries, clementines, dried fruits and nuts, fruits with cheese or cheese crackers, and alcoholic or non-alcoholic shaved ice drinks.

Check out Mahindi for frozen "Jungle Juice Slushy" and popcorn, nuts, chips, fountain beverages, and beer. Leaving Africa and heading into Asia, be sure to visit Mr. Kamal's, a vegetarian oasis featuring hummus, tzatzki salad (dressed with Greek yogurt, lemon juice, garlic, olive oil), and falafel, with fountain beverages.

Zuri's Sweet Shop

Sweet treats are all the rage at Zuri's, many of them with an animal theme. Cookies, candies, bins of bulk goodies, nuts, and snacks for everyone, healthy or indulgent, are on display. Check out the clever cake pops—cotton-top tamarin, grasshopper, and "Sahara Dessert"—or the zebra, giraffe, and hippo marshmallow pops.

Kusafari Coffee Shop & Bakery

DDP: No / Cost: $
TYPE: American; Quick Service; Snacks, Breakfast

This little counter is right next to Tusker House. Grab a cup of steaming coffee or cocoa and pair it with a Mickey-shaped cinnamon roll large enough for two to share. Breakfast wraps, Danish pastries, croissants, muffins, cereals, fresh fruit, and yogurt should prepare you for your trek through the Animal Kingdom. Later in the day, come back for paninis (smoked turkey, beef and cheddar, ham and cheese, tomato and mozzarella) sided with curry-spiced chips. Those breakfast pastries will still be around, and cookies, too. Lots of juices, fountain beverages, and coffee drinks (hot or iced) are always available at Kusafari.

Tamu Tamu

DDP: One credit (S) / Cost: $
TYPE: American; Quick Service; Snacks

Stop here if your party is looking for something cool, quick, and delicious. A chocolate waffle with vanilla ice cream or chocolate mousse on top, an ice cream/cookie sandwich, the always popular Dole Whip (with or without coconut rum or dark rum), chocolate-covered espresso beans, and many fountain beverages ought to cool everyone off on a warm day.

Harambe Market

DDP: One credit (Q) / $
TYPE: African; Quick Service; Snacks

Inspired by African street vendors, walk right up and place your order at the counter. You'll find chicken, beef and pork sausage, ribs, or a vegetable stack, sided with a black-eyed pea salad. Kids may want corn dogs or barbecue chicken or ribs. Harambe serves warm malva cake (of Cape Dutch-African origin, it contains apricot jam and has a spongy caramelized texture) for dessert. Alcoholic and non-alcoholic beverages are available.

Tusker House

DDP: One credit (T) / Cost: $$-$$$ (TiW)
TYPE: African; Character Unique/Themed; Breakfast, Lunch, and Dinner

A "tusker" refers to a large bull elephant, and Tusker House is a great place for you to interact with Donald Duck, Daisy, Mickey, and Goofy in their safari garb. There are parades through the restaurant and children are invited to march along. Characters will pose for pictures at your table and sign autographs. You'll find one of the nicest, most extensive selections of menu items at Tusker's bountiful buffet. Those in your group should be able to find plenty to keep them satisfied.

Breakfast fare is fresh fruits, pastries (warm cinnamon rolls, lemon poppyseed bread, croissants, etc.), eggs, meats, Mickey waffles, quiche, potatoes, oatmeal with toppings, cereals, African mealie pap, and the kitchen sink—almost! Lunch and dinner feature American and "African-inspired" selections like salmon, pork, spit-roasted chicken, potatoes, mac and cheese, corn dog nuggets, couscous salad, tofu, fruits and salads, cakes, cookies, brownies, and tarts.

Both children and adults will find much to celebrate here! It's one of the best dining experiences in the Animal Kingdom

Rafiki's Planet Watch

You've taken the narrow gauge Wildlife Express Train all the way out to see Rafiki, the wise bird from *The Lion King*. Chip and Dale may be there, too, dressed for a safari. You'll see animal conservation up close and personal, and guests can even touch some of the inhabitants here in the Affection Section. Your party will learn about behind-the-scenes care of the animals and have a chance to interact with staff veterinarians while viewing a real examination room. You'll see plenty of nutritious snacks on hand, ready to feed to the well-cared-for animals.

For the longest time, Rafiki's Planet Watch had no food or beverage stations for *human beings*, a puzzling omission since you've literally been tripping over kiosks, wagons, carts, quick-serve counters, and table-service restaurants from the moment you entered the park.

But that's changed. Rafiki's Planet Watch now has a single ice-cream cart. Try a frozen banana and cue the animal noises.

Your expedition through Disney's Animal Kingdom heads to Asia next, and then the newest land in the park, Pandora—the World of Avatar, before wrapping up at DinoLand U.S.A. The first part of this theme park was filled with fantastic places to dine. The second part doesn't contain nearly the variety of options; if you find yourselves at a loss as to where to eat, you might consider revisiting one of the relatively close restaurants in Africa, Discovery Island, or maybe the Rainforest Café on your way out through the Oasis. At this point in your trek, you will really begin to appreciate the sheer size of Animal Kingdom.

Disney's Animal Kingdom, Part Two

Asia, Pandora, and DinoLand USA

Asia

Asia Kiosks, Wagons, and Carts

Warung Outpost is one of the first things you'll pass in Asia traveling clockwise through the park. It's right outside the entrance to Flights of Wonder. Think chips, Mickey pretzels, and lots of drinks, both alcoholic and not. Margaritas and strawberry freezes are available, too.

Drinkwallah is situated on the water across from the Yak and Yeti Restaurant. Frozen Coke, whole fruits, and chips enjoyed in the shade ought to perk everyone up. Anandapur Frozen Beverages is in front of the bridge that leads to Discovery Island. Seasonal beverages will vary, and many come hot or iced, but frozen Coke with Captain Morgan Rum or frozen blue raspberry will keep you cool.

Chakranadi is located at the entrance to the Majarajah Jungle Trek well off the beaten path. It sells Mickey pretzels and glazed nuts, beer, and bottled beverages.

You can't miss the bright blue Adananpur Ice Cream Truck—and you shouldn't! (It's the last thing you'll pass before coming to the Thirsty River Bar on the way out of Asia heading for DinoLand.) Soft-serve vanilla, chocolate, or twist ice cream in a waffle cone, floats, and fountain beverages will cool you off on the warmest afternoon.

Thirsty River Bar and Trek Snacks

DDP: No / Cost: $
Type: Asian; Quick Service; Snacks, Breakfast, Lunch, and Dinner

Past the bright blue Anandapur Ice Cream Truck, you'll find this convenient place to pick up a snack on your way to Expedition Everest. This little kiosk tries hard to be all things to all people. At breakfast time, you can pick up a croissant or Danish. An oldie but goodie, the frozen banana (covered in chocolate and nuts), is back—and you can pick one up right here. Popcorn, ice cream treats, frozen juices, and all-day beverages are served anytime. For a quick meal, hummus with veggies and pita or Smucker's Uncrustables are available. Mickey pretzels, chips, and popcorn are, too. The drink selection is wide, and includes the Khumbu Icefall, the Flying Yak (non-alcoholic), and the Himalayan Ghost, to name just a few. Lots of beers, ales, and a few wines are sold at Thirsty River Bar, too.

Yak & Yeti Quality Beverages

DDP: No / Cost: $
Type: Chinese; Quick Service; Snacks, Lunch, and Dinner

Feel like you only have time for a grab-and-go snack or meal? Then this is your answer in Asia, though it might be a little hard to find. Look behind the Yak & Yeti Local Foods Cafés. It's not something you'd notice if you weren't specifically looking for it. Seating is outdoors. The cuisine is Chinese, the options are limited, but it will be fast and tasty, and sometimes that's just right. Specialty drinks like the Yak Attack or Frozen Emperor Margarita are popular choices. Lots of cold draft beers are on tap as well as Beso del Sol (Kiss of the Sun) sangria and the usual wide variety of fountain drinks and non-alcoholic beverages. Asian chicken sandwiches or a turkey leg with chips, egg rolls, and a ginger chicken salad are easily portable and will get you on your way to your next destination.

Yak & Yeti Local Foods Cafés

DDP: One credit (Q) / Cost: $
Type: Pan-Asian; Quick Service; Snacks, Breakfast, Lunch, Dinner

Maybe you don't feel like devoting the time to a lengthy, sit-down meal. Instead, try this open-air café for similar types of food without the wait, especially if you don't have a reservation at the Yak & Yeti Restaurant and you can't get a table as a walk-up. Continue past the restaurant and you'll see the exotic cafés that resemble those you'd find in remote parts of Asia. The cuisine is Pan-Asian, and most of it will be quite familiar to Americans: breakfast sandwiches, burritos, or tacos with eggs, cheese, bacon, sausage, and English muffins with sides of fruit salad and hash browns. For lunch or dinner, you'll see Kobe beef hot dogs or cheeseburgers, teriyaki beef bowl with white rice, ginger chicken salads, roasted vegetables couscous wrap, and honey chicken sandwiches. Many kinds of egg rolls and chicken fried rice are available as sides. Kids can pick from a pancake and sausage stack or French toast sticks, cheeseburgers, Smucker's Uncrustables, and chicken tenders. Try the mini mango pie, mini chocolate silk cake, or frozen lemonade for dessert.

Yak & Yeti Restaurant

DDP: One credit (T) / Cost: $$
Type: Asian-Fusion; Unique/Themed; Lunch and Dinner

Dine amid décor featuring genuine art and artifacts from the Nepalese region of Asia inside the lovely, cool Yak & Yeti. Despite the advertised "Asian-Fusion" cuisine, many of the menu items will be familiar, but among them you will also find some surprising, exciting combinations.

Appetizers (called "small plates") are pot stickers, firecracker shrimp, wok-fried green beans, and pork egg rolls. From there, move on to the "shareables," plates meant for two: lettuce cups (excellent), dim sum basket, ahi tuna nachos, and dragon roll. Specialties of the house are salmon, chicken, duck, and fish. Several kinds of wok-cooked dinners include sweet-and-sour chicken or pork, Korean barbecue ribs, and crispy honey chicken. In addition, there are many kinds of soups and salads, bowls of various noodles, and Kobe burgers, Korean barbecue ribs, or crispy coconut shrimp and steak. Popular choices like chicken, jasmine, brown, or house fried rice, and baby bok choy make nice sides.

Kids choose from among Smucker's Uncrustables, chicken tenders, mac and cheese, teriyaki chicken, cheeseburgers, mini corn dogs, and pork egg rolls.

Even the dessert list is extensive, ranging from good old New York cheesecake to pineapple upside-down cake to mango pie or fried cream cheese wontons with vanilla ice cream and skewers of fresh pineapple. No? Then how about chocolate pudding cake with raspberry sauce or fruit sorbet? They aim to please!

Pandora: The World of Avatar

The newest addition to the Animal Kingdom opened on May 27, 2017. The land is inspired by James Cameron's *Avatar*, released in 2009 and still the highest-grossing film to date. It consists of two attractions, the Avatar Flight of Passage and the Na'vi River Journey. On the first, you'll catch a ride on a banshee for a 3D viewing experience. The second is a a gentle glide down a mysterious river where plants glow with their own bioluminescence amid a lush, alien jungle. You can also hike through the unearthly Mo'ara Valley to glimpse floating mountains and glowing plants and animals. You'll find some new and fun places to eat here, both casual. There's a lounge with drinks and snacks as well as a quick-service restaurant with fare different from anywhere else in Walt Disney World. If you've never had passion fruit boba balls sitting on top of your food and drinks, get ready!

Pandora Kiosks, Wagons, and Carts

Pandora is just getting started, but you'll already find some unusual, one-of-a-kind snacks here. On the ACE Mobile Treats Cart, you'll find the new "fruits of Mo'ra" fruit bar, and some refreshing drinks like Zico watermelon raspberry coconut water or mountain berry blast. Even the Power-C vitamin water is dragonfruit flavored. Telyu gummi candy is supposed to be a source of protein for the inhabitants of Pandora, but this candy is all sugar—dragon fruit, lemon, and fruit punch—and looks like garden-variety grubs on a stick. Celia fruit gummi candy tastes suspiciously like earthly strawberries. Kids will have fun with them. Pandoran tree spores are actually just brownie bites covered with purple or blue coconut. The Expedition Trail Mix looks just like ordinary trail mix. The same goes for Pandoran sugar crystals on a stick. The blueberry almond popcorn is mostly notable because it's blue. One item to buy more for its looks than its flavor is the pretty Vein Pod—krispy treats have made their way across the galaxy. The pods are large enough to share and covered in white chocolate tinted green with lacy veins of regular chocolate. Don't expect to find churros and popcorn in Pandora.

Pongu Pongu
DDP: One Credit (S) / Cost: $
Type: Na'vi; Quick Service; Drinks and Snacks

Translated from Na'vi as "Party Party," Pongu Pongu is a tucked-away quick-service restaurant just across the walkway from the Satu'li Canteen. It's run by "a friendly expat" who visited Avatar and never returned. Find "out-of-this-world" drinks topped with pretty passion fruit boba balls. There are several non-alcoholic fruity drinks and many cocktails sold here, some of them glowing with their own bioluminescence, just like the plants you'll see here. Pricy souvenir mugs boost the price, but you get a glowing unadelta seed on top of your drink. A new treat to try here is the pongo lumpia, based on street food in the Philippines and Indonesia, that combines a sweet cream cheese and pineapple filling that's encased in a crispy, egg-roll-type outside. Pair them with Hawkes' Grog Ale, aka bright green beer, if you're feeling particularly adventurous.

Satu'li Canteen
DDP: One Credit (Q) / Cost: $
Type: Na'vi;. Quick Service; Lunch and Dinner

The restaurant resembles an old Quonset hut, a galactic outpost where you can refresh and refuel the members of your expedition. As soon as you arrive, try the latest My Disney Experience app on your iPhone or other mobile device to order your food, thus saving time waiting in line to place your order. Pay online, too. You'll receive a notification once it's ready, and you'll pick it up at the "Mobile Order Pick Up" sign. Because Satu'li Canteen is "owned and operated by Alpha Centauri Expeditons," the emphasis is on the fresh, natural bounty of Pandora.

Breakfast has recently been discontinued, but it's possible it might return during busy seasons. While it was being served, the offerings were simple, standard American fare.

Lunch and dinner mostly feature bowls with a protein (chicken, beef, fish, or cheeseburger bao buns), a grain, and a vegetable component . Mickey Check meals for kids are smaller versions of these, with "Teylu" all-beef hot dogs wrapped in dough or cheese quesadilla if the bowls are too exotic. It's worth noting that the vegetarian options are more creative than usual: chili spiced and crispy fried tofu or vegetable filled, steamed bao buns, both served with crispy veggie chips and veggie slaw with creamy dressing. Those fancy, colorful, other-worldly drinks from Pongu Pongu are on the menu here as well, in case you missed them.

Don't expect everything to look familiar on Pandora. The blueberry cream cheese mousse with passion fruit curd resembles a work of (Na'vian) art. The same goes for a gorgeous, rounded chocolate cake with banana cream, goji berries, and a cookie. Out of this world!

DinoLand U.S.A.

DinoLand Kiosks, Wagons, and Carts

On the path from Discovery Island to DinoLand, look for the Trilo-Bites kiosk. Buffalo chicken chips, turkey legs, smoky bones chocolate shake (with bourbon and candied bacon), ice cream floats, fountain beverages, soft serve ice cream (seasonally), and Sea Dog Sunfish draft beer should hold you over.

You'll find a cute stand called Dino Diner near the Fossil Fun Games. Grab something on the run from this counter that looks just like a 1950s trailer. Nachos supreme (loaded!), glazed nuts, chips, frozen Coke or lemonade, and other beverages, both alcoholic and not, are sold here, too. A popcorn stand is nearby, as well, and throughout DinoLand you'll come across several mobile ice cream carts.

Dino-Bite

DDP: No / Cost: $
Type: American; Quick Service; Snacks

At Dino-Bite, you'll find assorted flavors of Häagen-Dazs hand-scooped ice cream in a waffle cone, Edy's no-sugar ice cream, churros with chocolate sauce, a Bugs Sundae (ice cream, gummy worms, and cookie crumbles), hot fudge sundaes, cookies, chips, Mickey pretzels, and fountain beverages. This snack stop ought to keep the kids in your party, both big and the small, satisfied while visiting our prehistoric past.

Restaurantosaurus

DDP: One credit (S) / Cost: $
Type: American; Quick Service; Lunch and Dinner

Adjacent to the Boneyard, an archaeological dig, you can dine dino-style amid fossil replicas and "dig décor." The menu is designed to please most kids with Mickey Check meals—a Smucker's Uncrustable and a turkey wrap. There are other kid-friendly options, too, like chicken nuggets and cheese-burgers. Adults will find the typical array of Angus burgers, chicken dishes, chili-cheese hot dogs, and black bean burg-ers sided with fries, apple slices, or salad. Clam chowder is another option. For dessert, there are warm chocolate turtle brownies. Safari Amber, Bud Lite, or a Cretaceous Cooler with coconut rum, pineapple juice, and Midori (sweet, bright green Japanese liqueur) are served along with the standard fountain beverages, lemonade, chocolate milk, and juices.

Whether your safari here lasts one day, two days, or longer, you'll certainly cover a lot of territory in Disney's Animal Kingdom. The next and final theme park we have to explore is Disney's Hollywood Studios. The dining options there range from the sublime (relive the glory days of Hollywood at the Brown Derby) to the ridiculous but fun (Sci-Fi Dine-in Theatre, where you'll sit in modified convertible cars and eat while watching trailers for old science-fiction and horror movies)— and just about everything in between.

Disney's Hollywood Studios, Part One

Hollywood Boulevard, Echo Lake, and Muppet Courtyard

Tucked among several well-known, outstanding attractions and shows at Disney's Hollywood Studios, you'll find some equally outstanding places to dine. Sure, there are plenty of run-of-the-mill quick counters selling the usual nuggets, burgers, and fries, but there are also a few restaurants that will pleasantly surprise you. You just have to know where to look for them, and that's exactly what I'm going to tell you.

Hollywood Studios, the third of Disney World's four theme parks, opened on May 1, 1989. It's somewhat larger than the Magic Kingdom and considerably smaller than either Epcot or the Animal Kingdom. It comes in at about 135 acres and has the least regular footprint of them all, which makes getting around with any kind of organized plan a bit more challenging.

Echo Lake is intended to be the central "hub," but it's not quite that simple. Hollywood Studios is shaped something like the head of Oswald the Rabbit, one of Walt's earliest animated creations. Muppet Courtyard is his open mouth. His round face is comprised of Pixar Place, Commissary Lane, Animation Courtyard, and Echo Lake. Heading up one of Oswald's two long ears, Hollywood Boulevard, you'll encounter the Tower of Terror and Rock 'n' Roller Coaster. The other ear, really just a path, ends at the outdoor arena where the Fantasmic! show happens. There's no way to follow a regular clockwise route through *this* park, so we'll simply take it one area at a time.

Hollywood Studios has undergone several revisions (and a name change) since it opened and has been branded and re-branded over the years. The original affiliation with MGM has been dropped like a hot potato, due to a rather contentious parting of the ways. At one point, part of this park was an actual, working film studio. It's still in the process of finding a distinct identity, with the huge new Star Wars and Toy Story additions poised to take center stage.

On opening day, then-CEO Michael Eisner said:

> The World you have entered was created by The Walt Disney Company and is dedicated to Hollywood—not a place on a map, but a state of mind that exists wherever people dream and wonder and imagine, a place where illusion and reality are fused by technological magic. We welcome you to a Hollywood that never was—and always will be.

Nostalgia still plays an important role here, and California's idealized version of Hollywood during the 1930s-1940s is the period being celebrated.

Hollywood Boulevard

The first area to explore is Hollywood Boulevard, named for the original street in California. It's the main thoroughfare funneling guests into the rest of the park, a lot like Main Street, U.S.A., does in the Magic Kingdom. There's a replica of the Crossroads of the World statue as you enter the street, a nod to the first outdoor shopping mall on Sunset Boulevard. The original statue, however, doesn't have Mickey Mouse striding cheerfully atop the globe, but there's a lot of shopping here, just like the shopping center in California. This area is also a venue for parades and street performers. At the opposite end of the boulevard is an exact re-creation of Grauman's Chinese Theatre with hand and footprints of the movie stars in cement like the ones you've seen in all those old newsreel clips. On the boulevard, you'll also find a re-creation of the first Brown Derby restaurant, and it's one of the nicest places for lunch or dinner in the entire resort. Just don't expect to see Lucy and Desi sipping cocktails at the next table.

Hollywood Boulevard Kiosks, Wagons, and Carts

Past the main entrance, look for the red-and-white striped awning of the ICE COLD Coca Cola kiosk. Juices, a cherry slushy, Coke products, iced coffees, a variety of chips, chocolate chip cookies, Mickey ice cream bars, and ice cream sandwiches are available here.

At the fork where Sunset Boulevard meets Hollywood Boulevard, you'll find a well-stocked ice-cream kiosk loaded with Mickey bars, ice cream sandwiches, frozen bananas with nuts and chocolate, Nestle's orange cream bars, frozen orangeade, frozen lemonade, cotton candy, bananas, fountain beverages, and beer.

Glazed peanuts and almonds, ice cream bars, frozen fruit bars, Coke products, frozen lemonade, and beer are available at a little mobile cart on Hollywood Boulevard.

Three popcorn carts dot this area of the park. In addition to popcorn, they sell Mickey pretzels with cheese sauce, all kinds of Coke beverages, and some souvenir Star Wars steins.

A mobile pretzel and churro stand is usually found by the exit to The Great Movie Ride. In addition to Mickey pretzels with cheese sauce and churros, it usually carries whole fruit, Mickey ice cream bars, ice cream sandwiches, Coke beverages, Bud Light and Safari Amber draft beers, and Schöfferhofer Grapefruit Hefeweizen (a German beer).

The Trolley Car Café

DDP: One credit (Q) / Cost: $
TYPE: American;. Quick Service; Snacks and Drinks; Breakfast

Across the street from the Brown Derby, look for this quaint café on the corner of Hollywood and Sunset boulevards. It's a veritable Starbucks heaven, from the *two dozen* varieties of blended frappuccinos to the *almost two dozen* espressos. There's just one smoothie—strawberry. Refreshers, coffees, teas, and seasonal offerings galore round out this extremely robust drink menu. You can find delightful pastries from La Boulangerie to pair with your beverage. For breakfast, if you're hungrier than that, you can select a ham, egg, and Swiss croissant; a spinach, feta, and egg white wrap; or various breakfast sandwiches with meats, egg, and cheese. Later in the day, select from a roster of other choices: roast beef, pastrami, or turkey sandwiches, blueberry and cheddar salad, the infamous Darth Vader cupcake, a fruit tart, chocolate-covered brownie, cookies, and other goodies. Covered seating is available outdoors. This little café might be just what you're looking for. Save me a seat!

The Hollywood Brown Derby

DDP: Two credits (T) / Cost: $$$ (TiW)
TYPE: American. Fine/Signature, Lunch and Dinner

For the best, most elegant, as-close-as-it-gets taste of what old Hollywood was like, book a table at the Brown Derby. Service is impeccable. Menu selections are not only inventive but beautifully prepared and plated. The quality of the food is excellent. It's a splurge in every way, but this is one of the reasons why you came to Walt Disney World, for superlative dining experiences different from those available anywhere else.

Start with the crispy jumbo lump crab cakes, Cobb salad, roasted Zellwood corn soup, beef carpaccio, or ahi tuna crusted with togarashi (Japanese chili) and pumpkin seeds. Tempting lunch entrées like charred filet of beef, duck two ways (pan seared duck breast and duck confit), rack of lamb, a melt-in-your-mouth Wagyu burger, Faroe Island salmon, pan-seared grouper, Bell & Evans chicken, and several others will indulge your appetite. To add another level of indulgence, consider an "enhancement" to your entrée, such as a cold-water lobster tail, shrimp skewer, or Georges Bank seared sea scallops. Warm blueberry cobbler, a chocolate mascarpone sphere infused with apricot-orange jam, crème brûlée, banana toffee cake, or the elegant signature grapefruit cake will bring your meal at the Brown Derby to a memorable close. Haven't had Bananas Foster recently? No problem. You'll also find frappuccino brûlée, or a sinful dark chocolate cremeux with apricot marmalade and a white chocolate amber ring that's almost too pretty to eat—almost. Many premium teas are available as well as a nice selection of wines.

Children will dine every bit as decadently as the adults with their own fabulous menu. Even Mickey Check meals here raise the bar with pan-seared black grouper. Of course kids could instead opt for fish sticks and chicken noodle soup, grilled cheese sandwich, or a hot dog.

Two other special experiences happen here. You can get the Fantasmic! Dinner Package (first feast and then head to your reserved seats for Fantasmic!) or Dine with an Imagineer (four courses in the Bamboo Room), both of which are guaranteed to "wow" even the most blasé of guests. A seat at the Imagineer's table is about the most difficult reservation to get in the entire resort. Some try unsuccessfully for years. You must be over 14, it's only offered at lunch on Mondays, Wednesdays, and Fridays, and it seats no more than eight guests.

If you're going in style, this is the place to do it. Cut. Print.

The Hollywood Brown Derby Lounge
DDP: No / Cost: $
TYPE: American; Lounge; Snacks and Drinks

Couldn't get a reservation at the Brown Derby? No worries. You can try some of the same flavors here. It's a great chance to sit at one of the outdoor umbrella-covered tables, watch the people-parade go by, order a couple of small plates to share, and sample some of the specialty drinks this place excels at making. The artisanal cheeses and charcuterie board will surely amuse your taste buds. Tamarind-glazed pork belly, braised beef arepas (a maize-based dough used in South American cooking), andouille-crusted shrimp, the famous Cobb salad, and a trio of Derby sliders guaranteed to leave you star-struck are other delightful alternatives. Some of those great Derby desserts are offered, too, as a mini-trio sampler. The drink menu is outstanding. Specialty cocktails and martinis, premium ales and beers galore, flights (martinis, white wine, Pinot noir, and margaritas), and red and white wines by the glass offer you a veritable wealth of beverage possibilities. They also do a mighty good non-alcoholic Shirley Temple and No-jito for the kids.

Echo Lake

Echo Lake is a man-made lake in southern California, the backdrop for many early silent films. An aerial view of Hollywood Studios shows that its original design, later abandoned, incorporated the lake as one of Mickey Mouse's ears. It's still possible to see Mickey's two eyes and the suggestion of where a second ear would have gone from high above the park on Google Earth. Gertie, the dinosaur who stands in Echo Lake, was a vaudeville favorite, the animated subject of hand-painted films that influenced a young Walt Disney. Many of the buildings ringing the lake are similar to those once found in Los Angeles.

Hollywood Studios is undergoing some major construction projects as guests await the grand openings of Toy Story Land and Star Wars: Galaxy's Edge, but almost everywhere in the park you'll see new projects in progress. Echo Lake was drained for refurbishment shortly before Hurricane Irma hit in September 2017. Gertie got a spiffy new coat of paint. Lots of work has been done to get the huge new projection shows up and running. Disney Movie Magic celebrates the filmed history of the studio and is the first time Marvel characters are used in a Disney show here. At holiday time (November 9 through the end of December), you'll see the a "wowza" show: Sunset Seasons Greetings. Watch for the Christmas projections along the boulevard and on the Tower of Terror.

Echo Lake Kiosks, Wagons, and Carts

The Echo Lake ice cream cart, in addition to all the usual items, sells frozen bananas covered in chocolate and nuts, an Olaf strawberry lemonade bar, and frozen lemonade.

Dinosaur Gertie's Ice Cream of Extinction looks like a big, green brontosaurus and is an architectural nod to the many southern California buildings shaped like something unusual. Big oranges and donuts still dot the landscape. At Gertie's, you'll find soft-serve vanilla, chocolate, and twist...*when* it's open, that is. (It's only open during busy times.) Get it in a cup or a waffle cone. Mickey ice-cream bars and ice-cream sandwiches are sold here, too.

Peevy's Polar Pipeline is on Hollywood Boulevard near Echo Lake. Check out the refreshing frozen concoctions like Bacardi silver rum, Three Olives cherry vodka, and Jack Daniel's Tennessee whiskey. Non-alcoholic frozen drinks are Coke, blue raspberry, raspberry lemonade, wild cherry, and strawberry. Peevy's is also the spot for health-conscious snacks like carrot and celery sticks with lite ranch dip, whole pieces of fruit, pickles, grapes, and apple slices.

Funnel cake fans, get ready! Next to the Indiana Jones Stunt Spectacular is the little Oasis Canteen where you'll find funnel cakes topped with soft-serve ice cream and strawberries, cinnamon sugar, or powdered sugar. Try a refreshing root beer float or perhaps a Dreamsicle float made with Stoli vanilla vodka.

Backlot Express

DDP: One credit (Q) / Cost: $
TYPE: American; Quick Service; Lunch and Dinner

Made to resemble a studio backlot, compete with movie props, this quick stop is perfect for healthy alternatives to the usual park fare—although you'll find that here, too. Look for Backlot Express between Star Tours and Indiana Jones. It's huge, open-air, but covered from the elements. Lots of meals have a Star Wars theme, making this counter-serve extra cool.

The Dark Side chicken and waffles has Darth Vader waffles. The Royal Guard burger is served on a dark rye bun with barbecue beef brisket atop an Angus cheeseburger. A caprese sandwich and carrot sticks or a galactic chicken salad won't destroy your diet. Mickey Check meals are Smucker's Uncrustables or a Power Pack with yogurt. Kids meal choices also include the Darth Vader chicken and waffles. For dessert, Indulge with the sinfully delicious dark chocolate and peanut butter Darth Vader cupcake, chocolate mousse, or a BB-8 lemon cupcake with vanilla buttercream. Drinks are widely varied and include slushies, juices, fountain beverages, beers, wines, and margaritas. Look for souvenir Star Wars steins.

Min and Bill's Dockside Diner

DDP: One credit (Q) / Cost: $
TYPE: American;. Quick Service; Lunch and Dinner

This dockside diner is permanently docked on Echo Lake. It pays tribute to the 1931 film *Min and Bill*, starring Marjorie Dressler (who won the Best Actress Oscar for her performance) and Wallace Beery in the title roles. It won't offer some of the specialty dining experiences you can enjoy elsewhere in the park, and the menu is pretty limited, but the food is plentiful and reasonably priced, with chili-cheese dogs, a foot long dog, chili-cheese nachos, and pulled pork sliders. Milkshakes, fountain beverages, wines, and beers, or a frozen lemonade with a shot of Bacardi rum, are available.

50's Prime Time Café

DDP: One credit (T) / Cost: $$ (TiW)
TYPE: American; Unique/Themed; Lunch and Dinner

Another of the "don't miss" restaurants here at Hollywood Studios is this 1950's unique café. Find it near Indiana Jones and right across from Gertie, the dinosaur on Echo Lake. You'll feel like you've stepped into a black-and-white television program—and that's how you'll be treated. Oh, and by the way, you'll want to request being seated at one of the tables with a TV screen to experience the full 1950s effect. If being told to "eat your vegetables" or "get those elbows off the table, dear" doesn't bother you, jump into the spirit of the place and have a blast from the past! The décor is authentic mid-century modern, down to the last flying brass duck on the wall. With TV sets turned on and kitchen tables set, you'll find good, old-fashioned food prepared in traditional American style served by friendly wait staff who are part of the experience.

Start with beer-battered onion rings, a wedge of iceberg lettuce salad, or chicken noodle soup. Many items are called Dad's, Mom's, Cousin's, Grandpa's, or Grandma's famous or favorite recipe. Stuffed pork chops, fried chicken and mashed potatoes, meat loaf, pot roast, veggie lasagna, chicken pot pie, fish of the day, and salmon Caesar salad are just some of the entrées. If you've been good, think about rewarding yourself with warm apple crisp, Dad's brownie sundae, pineapple upside down cake, or maybe a big slice of Mom's famous chocolate-peanut butter cake for dessert—with ice cream, of course.

Kids will be just as happy as adults with their menu for four Mickey Check meals (salmon, baked chicken, turkey meatloaf, or meatless spaghetti) and items like mac and cheese, chicken pot pie, nuggets, or a hearty pot roast sandwich.

Just as intriguing as the food are the drinks. A PBJ milkshake, Ariel or Buzz punch, and Mickey's Bee Bop drink with glowing ice cubes in a souvenir cup are just a few. The adult beverages are equally enticing. Many red, white, and blush wines are listed, along with craft and draft beers, but it's the crazy cocktails that take center stage here in the 1950s. A Mowie Wowie, Dad's Electric Lemonade (it's neon blue!), or Grandma's Picnic Punch (that literally packs a wallop) will open your eyes.

Prime Time Café is one of those special dining experiences that Disney does so well. Don't miss out on this homage to 50s fun!

Hollywood & Vine

DDP: One credit (T) / Cost: $$ (breakfast), $$$ (lunch, dinner) (TiW)
TYPE: American; Character Buffet; Breakfast, Lunch, and Dinner

Breakfast at 8:00 a.m. means getting into the park early *provided* you are seated on time. Remember, you are guaranteed the next *available* table, not a table reserved for you and you alone at 8:00 a.m.

This charming diner is on the corner across from Echo Lake. Meet Princess Sofia, Jake from the Neverland Pirates, Handy Manny, Doc McStuffins, and other Disney Jr. regulars at breakfast. At lunch and dinner, Minnie and the whole gang will be here hosting themed holiday buffets.

Breakfast has serve-yourself American favorites like pancakes, Mickey waffles, eggs, potatoes, fruit, bakery treats, breakfast meats, hot and cold cereals, biscuits and sausage gravy, yogurt, and omelettes made to order. Lunch has create-your-own salads, seasonal carved meat stations, pasta, and seasonal fish. There is also a buffet area just for children. Soft-serve ice cream and an array of desserts are available. Dinner offers more choices than lunch and is slightly more expensive. You'll find peel-and-eat shrimp, turkey and stuffing, pasta, seafood mac and cheese, seasonal pork, ham, and holiday desserts.

If you aren't able to get a reservation for Cinderella's Royal Table, you may be able to get one here. The food is adequate, similar to most character buffets, and the characters themselves are always delightful.

Muppet Courtyard

PizzaRizzo

DDP: One credit (Q) / Cost: $
TYPE: Italian/American; Quick Service; Lunch and Dinner

Remember Rizzo the Rat, a Muppet character? (You might even remember the 1969 *Midnight Cowboy* character Ratso Rizzo who was Muppet Rizzo's inspiration.) He's the proprietor of this pizza establishment. Dine inside or out on the deck. If your kids crave mainstream-type Italian/American food, they'll find it here. It's no Via Napoli at Epcot's World Showcase, not by a long shot, but it will fill up the troops in a hurry with very little fuss. Meatball subs, pizzas, antipasto salads, and Mickey Check meals (mini-chicken sub or a yogurt Power Pack) are the main features. A limited beer selection and limoncello lemonade plus many non-alcoholic beverages fill out the drinks list. For dessert, there's cannoli and tiramisù.

Mama Melrose's

DDP: One credit (T) / Cost: $$ (TiW)
TYPE: Italian/American; Casual; Lunch and Dinner

Mama's is one of your best options for dining in Hollywood Studios. It's tucked behind the Muppet*Vision 3D Theatre in the Muppet Courtyard. The vibe is fun and old-time casual with plastic grapes and vines twined around the rafters filled with tiny lights. Book the VIP section for dinner and watch Fantasmic! over dessert and coffee. The menu is extensive enough to please nearly everyone's palate.

Appetizers are a big cut above average. Crispy calamari, vine-ripened tomatoes with fresh mozzarella, oak-fired mussels, and vegetarian minestrone are just some of the starters. Four crowd-pleasing flatbreads are great to share. Entrées range from standard Italian fare like spaghetti and meatballs, seafood cioppino, and chicken parmesan to the more adventurous saltimbocca, penne alla vodka, and shrimp campanelle. Desserts are Italian classics tiramisù, cannoli, and gelato, plus American favorites like strawberry cheesecake and Ghirardelli chocolate cherry torte. If you simply can't decide, order the dessert sampler for mini-versions of several.

Kids will find the usual Mickey Check meals: spaghetti, fish, and chicken. They can also order pasta and meatballs, chicken parm, or cheese pizza from the kids menu.

The wine list featuring Italian and California wines is extensive and pairs well with the food. Try the Bella wine flight or California gold wine flight with 2 oz. pours. Beers and liquors are also available. Non-alcoholic beverages are inventive. Specialty and dessert cocktails (Italian Surfer, Double Espresso Martini, and many more) are sure to please.

You've seen half of Disney's Hollywood Studios. Now, let's find out what the other half has to offer. As the second smallest theme park at the resort, it's relatively easy to see it all in a day.

Disney's Hollywood Studios, Part Two

Pixar Place, Commissary Lane, Animation Courtyard, and Sunset Boulevard

Pixar Place

The Pixar Animation Studios area in Disney Hollywood Studios is a smaller, representative model of Pixar's own studio in Emeryville, California. Pixar began in 1979 as the computer division of Lucasfilm. Back when the park opened and functioned as a production studio, the sound stages here were used in those productions. Now, they've been repurposed. It's a small area where you'll find Toy Story Mania! and not much in the way of dining options, aside from a few snacks.

Pixar Place Kiosks, Wagons, and Carts

While you won't find any full-service restaurants in Pixar Place, you won't go hungry, either. Joffrey's Coffee and Tea Company is a familiar façade at Walt Disney World and can be reliably counted on for good coffee, espresso, pastries, and tea. Seasonal beverages are usually available at Joffrey's.

Count on Hey Howdy Hey! Takeaway for quick snacks or even a grab-and-go meal like hot dogs and chips, Mickey pretzels, popcorn, frozen and fountain beverages, and pieces of whole fruit.

If ice cream is what you want, there's a cart selling Mickey ice cream bars, ice cream sandwiches, and frozen lemonade. Adults will find beer sold here.

A handy Snack Cart parked in Pixar Place will set you up with a ham and cheese-stuffed pretzel, churros (long, thin Mexican donuts), cotton candy, corn dogs, ice cream bars and sandwiches, Bud Lite, and Angry Orchard Crisp Apple Hard Cider.

Commissary Lane

There are two eateries on Commissary Lane. The first is intended to closely resemble the actual ABC TV Studio cafeteria where actors, directors, and crew rubbed elbows years ago. Its Deco style is authentic to the period. The second is a unique/themed dining experience, one you won't want to miss if you can help it. It's a trip back in time to an era when convertibles with enormous fins roamed the earth and drive-ins weren't yet extinct in southern California.

ABC Commissary

DDP: One credit (Q) / Cost: $
TYPE: American; Quick Service; Lunch and Dinner

Enter though a palm-lined promenade and step back into the golden age of television. Don't expect a lot of creative menu entries here. Watch vintage show trailers and see posters highlighting hit shows of the past. Props and wardrobe items are also on display. Ask about the allergy-friendly menu selections.

The commissary offers Kosher meals: hot dogs, corned beef, chicken strips, and beef burger come with potato croquettes. Kosher chocolate cake and apple strudel are the desserts. Non-Kosher choices include Angus cheeseburgers, Asian salad, Mediterranean salad (with chicken or salmon), a chicken and ribs combo, and a chicken club sandwich. Recently added to the menu are a lemon-pepper salmon, a chimichuri sirloin steak, and a Southwest burger. Mickey Check meals have the kids covered with a turkey sandwich or the Power Pack with yogurt. The kids menu features a cheeseburger as well barbecued chicken or salmon. Desserts are chocolate mousse, an Olaf cupcake, or a no-sugar strawberry parfait. There are many fountain beverages and a couple of nice Robert Mondavi wines.

While the food isn't at the pinnacle of park dining, it's just right if you're looking for something reasonably priced, fast, and reliably decent.

Note: For guests seeking additional Kosher offerings in the parks, check Kusafai at the Animal Kingdom, Liberty Inn at Epcot, or Cosmic Rays at the Magic Kingdom. (There's also the nearby Kosher Korner just off I-4—take exit 24, the Lake Buena Vista exit—under the rabbinical supervision of Chabad.)

Sci-Fi Dine-In Theatre Restaurant

DDP: One credit (T) / Cost: $$ (TiW)
TYPE: American; Unique/Themed; Lunch and Dinner

If you've made a reservation, this is such a cool place to eat; if not, *maybe* you'll get lucky with a cancellation. Sci-Fi Dine-in is popular for a reason. It's one of those special venues you and your group won't soon forget. Sit in modified 1950s convertible cars under the "stars" (little lights-in-the-ceiling variety) and watch great trailers of those famous old sci-fi and horror thrillers on the big screen that you *may* remember watching on late-night cable television during your childhood. The atmosphere is unique and the food is good, too.

Start with the fried dill pickles for a taste sensation. Spinach and artichoke dip is another tasty appetizer, as are the onion rings and spicy buffalo boneless chicken wings. Better yet, share the Sci-Fi Appetizer Sampler to taste 'em all!

The menu here is as "jumbo" as the fins on some of those classic cars. Just about anything your heart desires can be found on this menu. Chicken, salmon, pasta, build-your-own Angus burgers, St. Louis-style pork ribs, New York strip steak, shrimp, Reuben sandwich, Southwestern veggie burger, or the signature Drive-In BBQ Burger—you name it, Sci-Fi has it. Mickey Check meals are grilled salmon, grilled chicken, and wheat penne pasta. Kids menu items also offer popcorn chicken, cheeseburger, and mac and cheese.

Desserts are galactic-level good! The house-made candy bar is heavenly—white and dark chocolate mousse with crispy pearls between layers of sponge cake covered with chocolate ganache. The Out-of-This-World turtle cheesecake is equally amazing. What about a warm, glazed donut with cinnamon apples, vanilla-bean ice cream, and caramel sauce? If you have any willpower left, there's always the fresh fruit salad or the no-sugar added brownie and ice cream dessert.

Beverages are as imaginative and plentiful as the menu. Crazy cocktails with names like Magical Star Cocktail, Orbiting Oreos, Godiva Chocolate Martini, or Long Island Lunar Tea might intrigue the adults. No? Then how about a list as long as your arm of specialty draft, craft, and bottled beers? There are plenty of California wines and sangria, too. Joffrey's coffee and fun non-alcoholic beverages are available.

Don't miss out on a chance to visit a drive-in movie under the stars and sit in a vintage convertible, all the while dining on delicious menu selections. This is a very special Disney experience!

Animation Courtyard

When you see a large arch, you'll know you've arrived at Animation Courtyard, an area dedicated to the Disney animated films. In the early days of the park, this is where the backlot tours began. Now, you can see Disney Junior Live Onstage! with puppet characters from the Disney Junior Channel or a really fantastic live stage version of *The Little Mermaid*.

Animation Courtyard Kiosks, Wagons, and Carts

You won't find much in the way of food items in Animation Courtyard, so either eat up beforehand or wait until the next area, but there *is* an ice cream cart serving the ever-present Mickey ice cream bars, ice-cream sandwiches, Nestle's orange cream bars, strawberry fruit bars, frozen bananas covered in chocolate and nuts, frozen lemonade, and Coke products.

Sunset Boulevard

"All right, Mr. DeMille, I'm ready for my close-up," is the most famous line from the classic 1950 film *Sunset Boulevard*, directed by Billy Wilder and starring Gloria Swanson and William Holden. It was made into a Tony-winning musical in 1991 by Andrew Lloyd Weber. This area, a tribute to the famous street in California of the same name, represents the first major expansion of Hollywood Studios, in 1994. It's home to the incredible Tower of Terror, symbol of this park, and that wild ride known as Aerosmith's Rock 'n' Roller Coaster. It's also home to several places offering quick-service meals and snacks.

Sunset Boulevard Kiosks, Wagons, and Carts

A well-supplied Coffee, Espresso, and Pastries kiosk is at the exit from Tower of Terror. It'll meet your caffeinated pick-me-up needs, and maybe tempt you with some pastries as well. There are also two frozen beverages. Add a shot of Baileys, Kailua, or Jameson to a coffee or latte, if you're so inclined.

Hollywood Scoops is located in front of the Tower of Terror. Homey and quaint with its striped awning, it looks like those little places you'd have seen all over southern California in the 1930s and 1940s. Order hand-scooped ice cream (lots of flavors including sugar-free) served in a cone or a cup. Try warm apple crisp a la mode, a brownie sundae, fresh-baked cookie ice cream sandwiches, ice cream sundaes, or an alcoholic root beer float.

In front of Fantasmic! is an ice cream cart with those well-known Mickey ice cream bars, ice cream sandwiches, frozen lemonade, Coke products, plus three kinds of beer.

Next to the Rock 'n' Roller Coaster, look for a food truck called the KRNR Rock Station. Get a hot dog with chips to go, chocolate chip cookies, waffle cones, frozen Coke or lemonade, root beer floats, lots of Coca-Cola fountain beverages, some specialty drinks with alcohol, beer, and Angry Orchard Crisp Apple Hard Cider. Probably a good idea not to fill up on hot dogs before climbing on the roller coaster, though.

At Sweet Spells on Sunset near the Brown Derby, you can watch imaginative treats being created right before your eyes, including selfie-worthy candy apples, specialty cookies (Mickey's red shorts shortbread, large Mickey chocolate chip or peanut butter cookies), cake pops, chocolate-dipped strawberries, fudge in many flavors, English toffee, fancy peanut butter cups, mammoth pecan patties, and those whoppingly large whoopie pies (maple bacon! orange cream! cookies and cream!) that are currently sweeping the park with their popularity. There's a fresh pineapple skewer if you're forgoing sweets.

The following venues, taken together, are much like the famous Los Angeles Farmers Market. Hollywood Studios has five or six of these little stands, while the big Farmers Market boasts over one hundred, but the vibe is similar. It's a great place to hang out, kick back, and indulge your appetite.

Anaheim Produce

DDP: No / Cost: $
TYPE: American;. Quick Service; Snacks

Sure, you can get Mickey pretzels and the ubiquitous chur-ros and chips here, but this little produce stand specializes in healthy snacks. Fresh whole fruit, granola, hummus, carrot and celery sticks, fruit cups, tomatoes, grapes, pineapple, pickles, sweet potato chips, dried cranberries, trail mix, and more will give you an energy boost. Frozen lemonade, frozen margaritas, and frozen seasonal Coladas will keep you cool. Three kinds of cold beer and the many fountain beverages made by Coke are also sold at this modest little market here on Sunset.

Sunshine Day Café

DDP: No / Cost: $
TYPE: American; Quick Service; Lunch and Dinner

The sun only shines on very busy days, the only time you'll find this counter open. It replaced Toluca Turkey Legs. The limited menu includes turkey legs with chips or baked beans and corn, chocolate chip cookies, chips, and various beverages.

Catalina Eddie's

DDP: One credit (Q) / Cost: $
TYPE: American;. Quick Service; Snacks, Lunch, and Dinner

The real "Catalina eddy" is a weather phenomena that causes thick clouds and dropping temperatures after dark. It's most prevalent from April to September, often centered around Catalina Island off the southern California coast. This place is much nicer than the weather that inspires its name. Look for it on Sunset near the Tower of Terror and the Rock 'n' Roller Coaster. The offerings are simple: pizza (cheese, pepperoni, or meat lovers) and Caesar salads (one of them with chicken). House-made seasonal cupcakes or chocolate mousse will satisfy your sweet tooth. Mickey Check meals for the kids are Smucker's Uncrustables or the Power Pack with yogurt. There is a cheese pizza on the children's menu. For drinks, Eddie serves up Coke beverages, apple and orange juice, a slushy, hot cocoa, tea, or coffee, sangria, and various beers.

Fairfax Fare

DDP: One credit (Q) / Cost: $
TYPE: American/Mexican; Quick Service; Lunch and Dinner

If you haven't yet tried tasty empanadas (a half-moon shaped pastry enclosing a filling; the empanada has Argentinian origins), here's your chance. Order the beef empanadas with cilantro rice, black beans, and corn/tomato salsa. Equally good is the el pastor pulled pork sandwich with sweet plantains (a different kind of banana). If you're really hungry, get the generous fajita platter with chicken and pork. When they say "loaded" baked potato here, they aren't kidding—it weighs in at about a full pound! The Fairfax salad is definitely hearty with pulled pork, bacon, roasted corn, tortilla strips, and cheddar cheese topped with jalapeño ranch dressing. So is the foot-long chili-cheese dog. Kids menu items are turkey sandwiches or Smucker's Uncrustables. Chocolate mousse and seasonal cupcakes are for dessert, and as you may already know, cupcakes at Disney are seriously out of this world. Coke products and three kinds of beer, along with the usual coffee, tea, and cocoa complete the menu. The food at Fairfax is different, a cut above, and will give you an idea of what authentic Hollywood flavors really are.

Rosie's All American Café

DDP: One credit (Q) / Cost: $
TYPE: American; Quick Service; Lunch and Dinner

Rosie's current claim to fame is the fried green tomato sandwich. Cheeseburgers and nuggets are also on Rosie's menu. Kids can get turkey sandwiches, nuggets, or the Power Pack with yogurt. Desserts are seasonal cupcakes, strawberry shortcake, or chocolate mousse. Coke products, several beers, a sangria, coffee, tea, cocoa, juices, and milk are served. Other than the fried green tomato sandwich, most of the menu items are much like those found throughout the parks.

Way to go! You've successfully managed to navigate the many food options in all four of the Walt Disney World theme parks. If you made reservations six months ahead of time and got a table at the most popular places, great. If you didn't, there's always next time. Not only that, there are always *plenty* of great places to eat, whether you have reservations or not. Eating earlier or later than average will allow you to take advantage of the less busy off-hours. Don't forget to check for same-day reservation cancellations, too.

The unique snacks at the theme parks are part of what makes the Disney experience so memorable. Make sure to try some while you are here because you won't find them back home. Those unique/themed and fine/signature dining restaurants and character meals will linger in everyone's memories long after the vacation comes to an end.

There are still two more areas on Disney property you'll want to visit because the dining options there are so appealing. Turn the page and I'll tell you about the best places to eat on the BoardWalk and, in the chapter after that, Disney Springs.

Disney's BoardWalk
Disney Dining Off-the-Beaten Path

On July 1, 1996, Walt Disney World's BoardWalk Resort and entertainment area opened. It was designed by Robert A.M. Stern, former head of the Yale School of Architecture, to evoke the feeling of turn-of-the-last-century Coney Island in Brooklyn, New York, and Atlantic City, New Jersey. "BoardWalk," as it's used here, is not a figure of speech; the walkway is constructed of boards just like the originals on which it is based.

As the sun goes down, the lights and colorful façades of the buildings reflected in the water turn this place into a nostalgic, shimmering dream. If you have childhood memories of playing games of chance at the midway of your fair, they will come back to you on the BoardWalk. Share them with the next generation. Street musicians, balloon artists, magicians, and other performers add to the excitement and old-time ambience.

People promenade along the quarter-mile long, U-shaped boardwalk by the shores of Crescent Lake to shop, be entertained, or just people-watch. To do all of that, of course, guests need something to sustain them. The dining possibilities here have expanded over the last twenty-odd years, making this charming district a destination in itself.

BoardWalk Eateries

Ample Hills Creamery

DDP: One credit (S) / Cost: $
TYPE: American; Quick Service; Snacks

Ample Hills is a great name for this sweet shop selling a variety of the coolest ice cream flavors around (She Sells Seashells, Malty Salty Pretzel Punch, Lemon Sky, Nona D's Oatmeal Lace...and that's just the *beginning*) can be had in cones large or small (waffle, sugar, or cake) with M & Ms, chocolate chip, cookie, or pretzel toppings. You can also order a milkshake and chose your ice cream flavor—but it won't be easy!

Funnel Cakes

DDP: One credit (S) /Cost: $
TYPE: American; Quick Service; Snacks

Find the funnel cake vendor on the water side of the Board-Walk between Flying Fish and Big River. Get them fresh and hot! Top yours with ice cream, powdered sugar, or chocolate sauce. It's the perfect treat to savor while strolling along the lake. If you've never tried fried ice cream (yes, it's possible!), here's your opportunity. To complete the festive selections, there's cotton candy.

BoardWalk Bakery

DDP: One credit (Q) / Cost: $
TYPE: American; Quick Service; Snacks, Breakfast, Lunch, Dinner

This pretty bakery on the BoardWalk features items different from those you'll find in the theme parks. Breakfast pastries like the ludicrously rich and justifiably famous Jersey crumb cake, a cranberry-orange or blueberry muffin, and a buttery croissant will get you on your way quickly. Lunch and dinner include soups and side salads which are filling, as is the roast beef and salami sandwich with Provolone. Rather opt for a simple salad? No problem. Order a Caesar with chicken or an herb-grilled chicken and apple salad with mixed greens. Bakery specialties like the popular key lime tart, Oreo cupcake, Mickey tart, strawberry cupcake, or one of the many fancy specialties cupcakes should make those taste buds sing.

Big River Grill and Brewing Works

DDP: One credit (T) / Cost: $$ (TiW)
TYPE: American; Casual; Lunch and Dinner

If you are a fan of microbreweries that produce craft beers, Big River is the only one located on Disney property. Dine inside or under an umbrella table on the Boardwalk overlooking Crescent Lake. Prices are relatively affordable, especially when compared to a premier dining establishment like Flying Fish.

The jalapeño spinach cheese dip with warm chips or the beer-cheese soup comes highly recommended. A nice variety of quesadillas, nachos, and salads with chicken or salmon are offered as appetizers. On the entrée menu, you'll find plenty of great choices: chicken, pastas, steaks, a steak and shrimp combo, ribs, flame-grilled meatloaf, burgers (including a Kobe beef burger), blackened mahi mahi, and salmon. The meals are hearty and satisfying, and most are meant to go well with the beers on tap. What's for dessert? Chocolate confusion or New York-style cheesecake.

Drinks include the usual array of non-alcoholic beverage choices. Cocktails are just about anything you can think of: mojitos, margaritas, and a long list of martinis. Sangria and red or white wines are available, as well as red and white alternatives. There's a Southern Flier Light Lager beer, low in carbs and calories. Beer is taken *very* seriously here. Try the Gadzooks Pilsner, Steamboat Pale Ale, Summer Wheat, Rocket Red Ale, or Sweet Magnolia American Brown Ale. Each one is lovingly described. For example, the Steamboat Pale Ale is "a classic American-style Pale Ale with the distinctive pine and citrus character of its signature Cascade hops. Original gravity: 13.0 degrees, Plato Alcohol by volume: 5.5 percent, Bitterness units: 36." For beer and ale devotees, or anyone who wants a tasty, filling meal that won't break the bank, look no further than Big River Brewery.

BoardWalk Joe's Marvelous Margaritas

DDP: No / Cost: $
TYPE: American; Quick Service; Snacks

Look for the cheery red and white awning with a big, neon JOE'S over a huge margarita glass on the roof of a little stand on the water. That's BoardWalk Joe's! You'll find a few tables to sit and people watch or grab somethings to enjoy as you stroll along. Five varieties of frozen margaritas, piña coladas, or the Captain's Seaside Sensation (pineapple smoothie with a shot of Captain Morgan spiced rum) will be cool and refreshing after a long afternoon in the theme parks. Pair your beverage with nachos and cheese, a Mickey pretzel, or roasted nuts if you need a little something before dinner. There are non-alcoholic pineapple smoothies, too, and bottled soft drinks.

ESPN Club Sports Central

DDP: One credit (T) / Cost: $ (TiW)
TYPE: American; Unique/Themed; Lunch and Dinner

A 90-foot square HD television is always tuned to the sports channel at this bar and grill. Choose from varied starters like tuna nachos, loaded tots, pub nachos with shrimp, shrimp and avocado salsa, chili and seasonally inspired soups, club fries, and hot, medium, or mild ESPN "dingers," or wings. Burgers are the specialty here, and there are eight appealing kinds to choose from. Both hearty and lighter entrées dot this extensive menu. Fish of the day, turkey sandwich, fish and chips, Asian stir fry, seafood mac and cheese, and lots more should fill even the emptiest stomach. Cheesecake, warm bourbon-pecan brownie, "The Boston" (orange chiffon with "Boston" cream and chocolate-butter glaze) or the ultimate chocolate indulgence known as "The Wedge" will sweeten the deal. Kids are covered with Mickey Check meals like seasonal grilled fish or chicken. They might choose a cheeseburger or hot dog instead, and many would be thrilled to top off their meal with the "worms and dirt" cupcake. It's good, even though it might look yucky!

The list of non-alcoholic specialty drinks is imaginative and fun for the young and young at heart. Wines, many from California, are available as well as several kinds of draft beers. An intriguing part of the ESPN menu is the very long list of "Bigs & Frozen Bigs." Try a Grand Slam, Bloody Mulligan, Pom-Pom Margarita, or Captain's Mai Tai for a unique adult beverage.

Flying Fish

(See chapter 14, under "BoardWalk Resort.)

Trattoria al Forno

DDP: One credit (T) / Cost: $$ (TiW)
TYPE: Italian; Casual; Breakfast and Dinner

While the cuisine is Italian, there are plenty of menu items that most American palates will find just delightful. It's a popular spot (replacing celebrity chef Cat Cora's Kouzinna in 2014).

Breakfast offers the choice of eggs lots of ways, a breakfast pizza, a granola/yogurt parfait, a tower of pancakes, pastries for the table, a golden frittata, oak grilled steak and cheesy egg torte, or other equally filling dishes. The Mickey Check kids option is an egg-white spinach and tomato omelette or steak and egg with fruit.

No lunch is served, but come back at dinner for an immersion in the cuisine of Italy. Even the wine list is 100% Italian here. Antipasti offers Venetian mussels, fried calamari, caprese salad, hand-rolled gnocchi, or charcuterie. Four appealing pizzas are served. Next comes the main course, and the choices are extensive. Oak grilled strip steak, pasta alla carbonara, lasagne, pasta alla Bolognese, chicken parm, littleneck clams in white wine butter over pasta, seared sea scallops, polpetta gigante (giant meatball), and whole roasted fish of the day will please most diners. Enhancements, should you need them, are strip steak, shrimp, jumbo scallops, and a grilled chicken breast. Mickey Check meals for the children are grilled chicken or seasonal fish.

Desserts are a bit on the "mini" side (unusual for Disney) like "a spoonful of gelato" (and even if you assume they're talking about a *quenelle*, that's still pretty skimpy), "a lady finger" tiramisù, or a roasted white chocolate custard and "an amaretti cookie." Maybe you'd rather skip it or get dessert elsewhere.

After cruising the dining possibilities on the BoardWalk, your next stop is Disney Springs. Restaurants there come and go over the years, so what you found on your last vacation to Walt Disney World might have been replaced this time around. Some of the most exciting new restaurants in the entire resort have opened recently at Disney Springs. Sure, the shopping has always been special here, but now the eating establishments are just as special. Try to make time for a visit! You won't regret it.

Disney Springs, Part One
Marketplace and The Landing

Many places and attractions at the resort have undergone several iterations and have managed to successfully reinvent themselves. Disney Springs is no exception. On March 22, 1975, during the resort's fourth year, this shopping and entertainment area opened as the relatively modest Lake Buena Vista Shopping Village. Lake Buena Vista is the mailing address for Florida's Disney operations. Before the land was bought by the Disney organization in the 1960s, it was known as Black Lake. Buena Vista Distribution Company was founded in 1953 by The Walt Disney Company after the release of *Peter Pan*. The Walt Disney Studios in Burbank, California, are located on Buena Vista Street. You'll see the Buena Vista name used by Disney again and again. It means "good view."

By 1977, the area was renamed Walt Disney World Village. Another name change came in 1989: Disney Village Marketplace. Early names put the focus squarely on shopping. That's no longer true. In 1989, the name was more reflective of the multi-use nature of the venue: Downtown Disney. What is now The Landing was then Pleasure Island, an adult-centered bar and entertainment center. Yet again, in 2015 after considerable expansion that added two parking structures and 150 new tenants, the area is now called Disney Springs. It is currently comprised of four areas with over 100 shops and stores and over 55 places to eat.

Marketplace

The Ganachery Chocolate Shop

Find "sophisticated" chocolate, ganache, and spirits at this attractive shop filled with every kind of chocolate imaginable. You can even discuss the merits of each with one of the resident chocolatiers on the scene. You'll be assisted in selecting something specially suited just to your taste. Watch the in-house magic happen in the kitchen where things are freshly prepared. Disney character-themed chocolate lollipops are available, along with a wide assortment of many people's favorite kind of candy—chocolate!

Goofy's Candy Company

You can either design your own individually prepared sweet treat or select from those already on tempting display in the cases and on the shelves. The candy apples are giant, adorably decorated, and sure to please. They resemble a rotating cast of characters like Olaf the Snowman, the Cheshire Cat, Mickey in *Fantasia*, Mike from *Monsters, Inc.*, Maleficent with horns in her dragon form, and of course, Goofy. The Goofy's Glaciers section has frozen slushy drinks you can blend to suit. They're not only beautiful and bright but the *perfect* cooler on a hot day. Candy galore in many gorgeous forms is what this store is all about. Even if you don't have a sweet tooth, you'll enjoy seeing the artistic culinary creativity on display. There's a large cut-out Goofy figure saying "Gawrsh, Thanks!"as you exit. No, Goofy, thank YOU!

Aristocrepes

DDP: No / Cost: $
TYPE: American; Quick Service; Snacks

You'll find sweet (s'mores, strawberries Romanov with brandy, or banana chocolate hazelnut) and savory (beef and cheese) crêpes and a selection of wines, beers, alcoholic sodas, and non-alcoholic beverages at this kiosk. For something unusual, try those fancy new "bubble" crepes—strawberry or salted caramel.

B.B. Wolf's Sausage Co.

DDP: No / Cost: $
TYPE: American; Quick Service; Snacks

Get it? The Big Bad Wolf is selling sausages! Bavarian, sweet/
hot, Portuguese, Italian/veggie, and a sampler of sausages all
come with house-made pickles. The "house" with its counter
looks like it could have come straight out of the old story.
Draft beer and fountain beverages are sold.

The Daily Poutine

DDP: No / Cost: $
TYPE: American; Quick Service; Snacks

What's poutine, you may be excused from wondering? It's
a homey dish that originated in Québec Provence in Canada.
Fries are the base, topped with cheese curds and a light brown
gravy. Although popular in Canada and sold in some northern
areas of the U.S., it's still an uncommon treat, especially south
of the Mason-Dixon Line. Classic, Latin, Italian, and French
versions of poutine are offered, along with beer, sangria, and
fountain beverages.

Dockside Margaritas

DDP: No / Cost: $
TYPE: American; Quick Service; Drinks

Many varieties of margaritas on the rocks or frozen, beer,
wine, hard cider, and a limited selection of non-alcoholic
drinks are available.

Ghirardelli Soda Fountain and Chocolate Shop

DDP: No / Cost: $
TYPE: American; Quick Service; Snacks

Your sense of smell might lead you to Ghirardelli's, but if not,
it's next to the World of Disney shop. Sundaes like you've
never had them before are the order of the day. They come
with toppings galore and have imaginative names: Earth-
quake, Cressy Field, Ocean Beach, Presidio Passion, Golden
Gate, Treasure Island, Strike it Rich, and others. Try one of
the Painted Ladies for an intensely dark sundae: Midnight
Reverie, Espresso Escape, or Mint Bliss. Shakes and floats,

scoops and cones, and sweet treats will leave everyone loosening their belts. Hot chocolates, hot, cold, and frozen beverages, and classic coffee drinks are on the menu. Want to take something home? Check out the shop filled to the rafters with Ghirardelli chocolate goodies.

Joffrey's Smoothies

DDP: No / Cost: $
TYPE: American; Quick Service; Snacks

The popular Joffrey's may be found in many locales at Walt Disney World. This little stand serves a tremendous variety of smoothies blended with Dippin' Dots vanilla yogurt and Minute Maid juice. Juices, coffee with Kahlua, Baileys, or Jameson, and tea with vodka and lemon are sold.

Starbucks

DDP: No / Cost: $
TYPE: American; Quick service; Snacks

Starbuck's favorites like frappuchino, espresso, latte, smoothies, iced coffee, tea, refreshers, and hot chocolate are on the menu at this walk-up counter, in sizes grande (16 oz.), venti (24 oz.), or trenta (30 oz.). Try adding a flavor or shot of espresso.

Wetzel's Pretzels

DDP: No / Cost: $
TYPE: American; Quick Service; Snacks

Across from World of Disney is a little stand where you can find delicious, fresh, warm pretzels. Get "sinful cinnamon" or "almond crunch," or try the baked cheese and pepperoni pretzel. For dipping, Wetzel's provides jalapeño or cheddar cheese, pizza, and sweet caramel sauce. Still hungry? Order a hot dog or cheese dog with lemonade, frozen lemonade, or frozen granita.

Earl of Sandwich

DDP: One credit (Q) / Cost: $
TYPE: American; Quick Service; Breakfast, Lunch, and Dinner

The fourth Earl of Sandwich, busy at the card table and reluctant to leave for a meal, slapped a piece of meat between two pieces of bread and invented the menu item that's been popular ever since. This extremely busy and highly popular restaurant was founded by the eleventh Earl of Sandwich, John Montagu, his younger son also named John Montagu, and businessman Robert Earl, who was the founder of the Planet Hollywood franchise. You'll find the restaurant near the Once Upon a Toy shop.

Breakfast sandwiches, fresh fruit yogurt, oatmeal, muffins, and made-to-order omelettes are served until 11:00 a.m. Lunch and dinner feature lots of familiar sandwiches as well as some original creations like the Full Montagu (beef, Swiss, turkey, and cheddar), Holiday Turkey (turkey, stuffing, gravy, and cranberry sauce), and Chipotle Chicken Avocado. Freshly tossed salads (Cobb, chicken Caesar, Greek, Thai chicken) are available, with many add-ons. Try the hand-crafted wraps and artisanal soups, too. Sides are mac and cheese, coleslaw, chips, potato, and pasta salad. Kids have a long menu of their own with plenty of appealing choices. Smoothies, fountain beverages, and sweets like cookies, brownies, strawberry shortcake, cupcakes, and frozen bananas are available. The Earl has something for everyone, including a "lite" menu called the Skinny Earl.

Wolfgang Puck Express
DDP: One credit (Q) / Cost: $
TYPE: American; Quick Service; Breakfast, Lunch, and Dinner

Located beside the Days of Christmas shop, Wolfgang Puck will gladly satisfy your need for a meal. You'll find modern, clean lines, and the illusion of eating in a chef's kitchen that just so happens to be well-equipped with plenty of tables. This place makes a point of using fresh, locally sourced ingredients, and the menu reflects a commitment to tasty, good food choices.

At breakfast, order spinach and mushroom omelette, breakfast pizza, breakfast sandwich, Belgian waffles, cornflake-crusted French toast with fresh fruit, or the "classic": scrambled eggs, bacon or sausage, crispy potatoes, and sourdough or wheat toast. The lunch and dinner menu substantially expands the possibilities. Soups are butternut squash with cardamom cream or chicken noodle with carrots and chives and the chef's seasonal selection. Salads, sandwiches (how about bacon-wrapped meatloaf with garlic aioli, crispy onion rings, and house-made chips?), and of course, plenty of pizzas and pasta will make nearly everyone happy. If you want more choices, consider entrées like chicken, crispy chicken tenders, more of that bacon-wrapped meatloaf sitting on mashed potatoes and topped with crispy onion rings, or roasted salmon with veggies. Desserts are fresh fruit cup, brownies, cookies, crème brûlée with berries, cheesecake, and frozen yogurt.

Rainforest Café

DDP: One credit (T) / Cost: $$
TYPE: American; Unique/Themed; Lunch and Dinner

Find this themed restaurant next to the Art of Disney shop. Other than not serving breakfast, it's similar to the one at Disney's Animal Kingdom. Refer to chapter 12, under "The Oasis," for a full description.

Rainforest Café Lava Lounge

DDP: One credit (Q) / Cost: $
TYPE: American; Casual; Snacks, Drinks, Lunch, and Dinner

The Rainforest Café Lava Lounge is situated in a gorgeous, peaceful spot on the water at the far end of the Marketplace. You'll access the outdoor covered seating area (right on the lake) through flowing magma inside a "lava tube" near the lounge's entrance. Water cascades down the rocks outside, a croc is poised to snap, and a tall volcano belches fire. Order the Awesome Appetizer Adventure for three (or more), margherita flatbread, crab dip, buffalo honey garlic wings, and lava nachos for two. There are many creative specialty cocktails for your pleasure. Try a tropical Cheeta Rita, Rainbow Colada, or a Mongoose Mai Tai. If you were unable to get a table in the actual Rainforest Café itself, always busy, you can still order off the regular menu here at the Lava Lounge. This is a cool place (plenty of fans blowing) to sip a drink, share an app, and relax from your busy day at the parks or shopping at Disney Springs.

T-Rex Café

DDP: One credit (T) / Cost: $$
TYPE: American; Unique/Themed; Lunch and Dinner

One of two locations, the other in Kansas City, your dino-happy kids will think they've landed in prehistoric times as they enter this themed café. It's an exciting, educational restaurant with interactive, hands-on activities and lots of life-sized dinosaurs that seem almost alive. The themed dining rooms are incredible. Check out the ice cavern with its frozen mastodon, Jurassic fern forest with huge buzzing wasps, and a gigantic, moving octopus in the "underwater" bar. Watch for the meteor shower that happens every twenty minutes. Be sure this isn't going to frighten your youngest party members because the illusion is very real. In addition to the restaurant, there's also an attached shop stocked with dino-themed merchandise.

For appetizers, start off with nachos, mozzarella sticks, bruschetta, flatbread, or the Supersaurus Sampler (for four) if you can't decide. The menu items, of course, have dinosaur names, but you'll recognize the food. Plenty of soups, salads, and pastas will appeal to both grown-ups and children. (Don't think you need to be with kids to thoroughly enjoy this fascinating venue.) Add onion rings, shrimp, or St. Louis-style spare ribs to your entrées. Good old burgers and sandwiches with names like Bronto Burger, Guac-asaurus, and Pork-asaurus are available. For the carnivores among your party, try NY strip steak, St. Louis ribs, or chicken. Seafoods such as shrimp, fish and chips, and salmon can be supplemented with add-ons. Red-skin potatoes, waffle fries, coleslaw, cinnamon apples, seasonal vegetables, chips, or "raptor" rice will all help fill up the ravenous members of your pack. Kids are covered with appealing goodies like corn dogs, shrimpkens, cheesy mac, lava lasagne, or paleo pizza. If they still aren't full, there's always the Chocolate Tarpit or Sabertooth Sundae for dessert.

As you might imagine, even the desserts here are dino-sized. How about an Ice Age for Two (layers of ice-cream sandwiches, hot fudge, whipped cream, and toffee bits)? Sorbet Sampler, Cosmic Key Lime Pie, Chocolate Extinction (enough for four or *more*), or meteor bites (donut holes with sauces for dipping) for two will surely sweeten the meal deal at T-Rex. This is a very popular venue, so don't neglect making those key reservations!

The Landing

Erin McKenna's Bakery NYC

DDP: No / Cost: $
TYPE: American; Quick Service; Snacks

Known as the world's premier gluten-free bakery, Erin's is an excellent example of how you can combine both good taste and vegan and gluten-free treats. She makes cupcakes, tea cakes, cookies, donuts, and more. You can also get just cupcake tops, a frosting shot, or cake bites if all you want is a taste. Look for Erin's cookbooks and other merchandise sold here as well.

Florida Snow Company

DDP: No / Cost: $
TYPE: American; Quick Service; Snacks

This little kiosk is between The Landing and the Marketplace, near Paddlefish. You can order shaved ice (snow cones) in lot of sweet flavors/neon colors and two sizes. You'll also find fresh roasted cinnamon glazed or salted nuts, and bottled beverages. What a perfectly cool snack for a hot day.

Jock Lindsey's Hangar Bar

DDP: No / Cost: $
TYPE: American; Quick Service; Snacks

This place looks like a plane hanger turned dive, but it's got a fantastically cool vibe. Who's Jock Lindsey? He's a friend of Indiana Jones, and the pilot who gets Indy out of some close shaves. He has a pet snake named Reggie and two planes, *OB1* and *OB-CPO*, in a not-so-veiled reference to George Lucas' *other* famous franchise. You can sit on the proprietor's boat docked outside named the *Reggie* in honor of said snake. You can even sit in an actual diving bell. The bar's decorated with memorabilia from Jock's many travels and adventures. Jock's that quintessential he-man all the guys want to *be* and all the women want to be *with*. Pull up a seat, get some tasty apps, and order something tall and cold.

The names of the snacks are as creative as can be: Wu Han's Hot Wings, Incan Tuna Tacos, Air Pirate's Pretzels, Fräulein's Flatbread, and Temple Tenderloin, to name just a few.

Seasonal specials such as Marshall College Flatbread (Indy's place of employment), Glider Sliders, and the Kali Ma Garita and Donovan's Dilemma to wash them down are sometimes available. Try a "Jocktail" at happy hour or order one of the numerous signature alcoholic libations with descriptive and colorful appellations. Here are a few: the Scottish Professor, German Mechanic, Bedtime Story, Wrong Island!, and Fountain of Youth. Non-alcoholic beverages include the Poisonless Dart, Diving Bell, Antidote, and Teddy's Tea. Look for wines galore, Épernay champagne and Veneto prosecco, beers and hard cider, a flight of whiskey, and even sake.

Tea Traders Café by Joffrey's

DDP: No / Cost: $
TYPE: American; Quick Service; Snacks

Premium iced teas, frozen tea or lemonade, spirited beverages hot or cold, black teas, loose leaf teas sold by the 2-ounce bag, a pu'erh chocolate-flavor tea, oolong teas, green teas, herbal and rooibos teas, and white teas will surely be enough to put tea lovers in a tizzy trying to decide among the many options. Then, of course, there's the decision about what to have *with* your cuppa. Several kinds of cookies (some tea flavored), cheesecake, and brownies are usually available.

Vivoli il Gelato

DDP: No / Cost: $
TYPE: American; Quick Service; Snacks

Choose gelato or sorbetto from a delightful list of flavors. Try a "waffle brown sundae" or a gelato or sorbetto float or milk shake. The four kinds of paninis available during busy seasons are petite, so you can buy one, two, or three of them. Lots of biscotti for dipping into drinks are made fresh daily, as are tortine (tarts) that come filled with a variety of Italian ingredients. Coffees like Americano, macchiato, cappuccino, latte, espresso, and doppio (a double espresso), iced tea, Coke products, and Italian sodas are available here as well.

Cookes of Dublin

DDP: One credit (Q) / Cost: $
TYPE: American; Quick Service; Breakfast, Lunch, and Dinner

In years past, Ireland wasn't famous for its cooking, but that has all changed—and for the better. Cookes, located near Raglan Road Pub and Restaurant, is well known for its excellent food and hospitable service. Enjoy your meal indoors or outside under the umbrellas bearing the Cookes name.

Light, crispy "day boat" selections make a fun lunch choice. Battered fish, shrimp, and Irish-style sausages are served with chips—*chips*, meaning hand-cut fries. The savory pies are different and delicious, either the beef and lamb or the chicken with field mushrooms. Burgers with *chips* and fresh salads will appeal to most American palates. Anyone in your group game to try the "Hog in a Box" for supper? It's slow-roasted pork shoulder with baby potatoes, sage and sweet onion stuffing, and apple sauce. A nice selection of side orders is offered including delicious Irish vintage cheese and bacon dip, mushy peas (you might find yourself pleasantly surprised), and double battered onion rings. Desserts are fresh and light, like the ice cream or Jammy Dodger Cookie, or dense and sinfully rich, like the peanut butter and chocolate chip or the orange chocolate pillow cookies. The food here is a big cut above average. So is the Irish-style live entertainment. Bring on the shamrocks!

The BOATHOUSE

DDP: Two credits (T) / Cost: $$$ (TiW)
TYPE: American/Seafood; Fine/Signature; Lunch and Dinner

Dine dockside in this popular venue surrounded by beautiful "dreamboats" from the 40s, 50s, and 60s. You can also take an Italian water taxi and tour the lake and waterfront. Make a splash in a vintage amphicar (amphibious automobile—yes, these were real vehicles, and they *didn't* belong to James Bond) or ride the nineteenth-century *Lady Rose* while sipping champagne and nibbling daintily on chocolate strawberries. If you're up for this adventure, book a Venezia Champagne Cruise for 30 or 60 minutes on the 40-foot-long Italian water taxi. As you might well imagine, none of these experiences comes cheap. In fact, quite the reverse. The food at the

BOATHOUSE is described as "Florida Surf and Turf." Like the boat rides, eating here doesn't come cheap, either.

The Captain's Raw Bar has oysters on the half shell, lobster cocktail, yellowfin tuna poke (a raw fish salad of Hawaiian origin), and wild Pacific shrimp. There are two more bars, the Admiral's Club Bar and Dock Bar. Chopped, wedge, Caesar, and garden salads are served. "Buckets" with fried fish, clam strips, or coconut Baja jumbo shrimp and fries are another option. Entrées of the sea (lobster, salmon, swordfish, ahi tuna), the sea *and* shore (lump crab, ribs, chicken, seafood mac and cheese, baked and stuffed lobster, pasta), sandwiches (lobster roll with a full Maine lobster, burgers, filet mignon sliders), and steaks (certified USDA blue-star heritage Angus), chops, and provisions provide practically anything you might want for lunch or dinner. There are more sides than you can shake a stick at—truffle fries, broccoli, roasted corn on the cob, asparagus, and more. If you can find room, there's key lime pie in a Mason jar, whiskey/caramel cornbread cake with stone fruits, s'mores baked Alaska, and several others to tempt your sweet tooth.

Chef Art Smith's Homecomin'

DDP: One credit (T) / Cost: $$ (TiW)
TYPE: Southern/American; Casual; Lunch and Dinner

The point of this delightful restaurant is to make you feel like you've somehow come upon a church supper in full swing or maybe wandered into Grandma's cozy kitchen. Look for it between STK Orlando and Morimoto Asia. It's "down home" cooking with a definite Floridan flair. There's an emphasis on fresh, local, and satisfying in every sense of the word.

The menu is highly descriptive. Church lady deviled eggs, bunch of puppies (hush puppies, that is), thigh-high chicken biscuits drizzled with hot honey, and "Ham, Ham, and Jam" on drop biscuits are just a few of the starters. Pork, chicken, and fish sandwiches are served with barbecue chips drizzled with ice box dressing. One entire menu section is devoted to "salads and dumplings"! For entrées, chicken and donuts, pork barbecue, fried catfish, shrimp and grits, and several others will remind you of home—assuming you had a fabulous chef in the family, and lived in the South. Art's signature fried chicken (brined in buttermilk for 24 hours) comes "served with creamy mashed potatoes, cheddar biscuits, and love." Sides are likewise plentiful. You can't leave without trying a real Southern dessert like hummingbird cake (said to be so sweet it attracts those pretty little birds), pecan pie, key lime pie, or Art's own famous shine cake—moonshine, that is. You'll be glad you came!

Morimoto Asia

DDP: One credit, lunch (T), Two cr., dinner (T) / Cost: $$-$$$ (TiW)
TYPE: Pan-Asian; Fine/Signature; Lunch and Dinner

Iron Chef Masaharu Morimoto works his brand of culinary magic here at The Landing, not far from Raglan Road. His newest restaurant is popular and packed, so if you hope to dine here, make a reservation in advance, although it's certainly possible to squeeze in at the last minute if you're feeling lucky and can scoop up someone's cancellation. The soaring, two-story ceilings with their twenty-foot-long sparkling chandeliers are breathtaking. There's a kitchen stage where you can watch dishes being prepared, intimate dining spaces, a lounge, and a sushi bar on the second story with its own entrance. The chef creates stunning and clever flavor combinations with foods from China, Japan, and Korea. Regardless of your personal preferences, if you enjoy Asian food, you'll find something delightful here.

The lunch menu is slightly less extensive than dinner, but it's similar. For starters, try edamame, rock shrimp tempura, hamachi tartare, or tuna pizza, among others. Dim sum is a small plate of something wonderful. Egg rolls, pork or chicken bao, pork or chicken dumplings, and many others are available. Sushi rolls range from the usual California to the unusual "spider" or barbecued eel and avocado rolls. Soups and salads, noodles and rice, spare ribs, and entrées featuring seafood, chicken, pork, veggies, and beef will leave you wondering how to pare down all those tempting choices. If you've never tried it, order Morimoto Peking Duck (for two)—a carved house-roasted whole duck with steamed flour pancakes, apricot sweet chili, and hoisin miso. From non-alcoholic drinks like the Blushing Dragon or Morimoto Punch to wine by the glass, cocktails like a Morimotini or Tom Yam

Siam, beers, and sake, you'll find plenty of fantastic beverages to accompany any meal selection. Desserts are available and range from the prosaic (churros) to the sublime (Mochi Mochi), providing you have room for anything more. Morimoto Asia is a welcome addition to Disney Springs!

Morimoto Asia Street Food

DDP: One credit (Q) / Cost: $ (lunch)-$$ (dinner)
TYPE: Pan-Asian; Quick Service; Lunch and Dinner

Want to sample the famous flavors of a Morimoto meal without the reservation or substantial investment? Grab some quick and savory snacks, noodle dishes, sushi, yummy bao tacos (pork, chicken teriyaki, or short rib in a soft steamed bun), and plenty of signature drinks. It's Asian street food, yes, but it's prepared in high style and tastes amazing.

Paddlefish

DDP: One credit (T) / Cost: $$ (TiW)
TYPE: Seafood/American; Casual; Lunch and Dinner

Climb aboard an old-fashioned paddle-wheeler and dine right on the water. This restaurant was formerly Fulton's Crab House, and now it's named after a freshwater fish only a mother could love, the homely, humble paddlefish.

Appetizers are fun here. Dinner has a wider selection than lunch. Try crab fries, a lobster corn dog, Maine mussels, charred octopus, crab cakes, calamari, beef skewers, or fried green tomatoes. Conch chowder and New England clam chowder are the soups, or you can try green and wheat berry salads. Add chicken, shrimp, or salmon to a salad for $3. There are chilled, raw seafoods including raw oysters piled high in an impressive $70 tower that serves four. Crab and lobster entrées come with farmer's market corn and new potatoes. Bass, salmon, scallops, catfish, jambalaya, fish and chips, and lots of other tempting treats "from the bay" are available. Steaks, burgers, short ribs, lamb, chicken, and pork join the seafoods. If you want something different, consider a specialty Low Country boil, a New England boil, an Alaska boil, or a Cracker boil. The list of sides is immense. Blistered green beans, sweet potato fries, mac and cheese, asparagus, and *lots* more to share will go very nicely with the entrées. Desserts are "down home" style: charred carrot cake, a brownie milkshake, donuts and coffee, key lime, strawberry shortcake, and a truly killer chocolate-bourbon-pecan tart with candied bacon, sea salt, and dulce de leche ice cream.

Paradiso 37

DDP: One credit (T) / Cost: $$ (TiW)
TYPE: North, Central, and South American Street Food; Casual; Lunch and Dinner

Paradiso 37 is adjacent to the Hangar Bar, right on the water. Dine inside and gasp at the impressive Tequila Tower or watch the boats go by outside while you sit under an umbrella on the deck and enjoy a cool breeze off the lake. This place is loud and lively! The popular bar is sure to be hopping at night.

The eats span the Western Hemisphere. South American crazy corn comes fire-roasted with cheese. Barbecued beef quesadillas, Colombian arepa cakes with roasted pork, or loaded nachos will start the party off right. Platters of the Americas include grilled salmon, Baja fish tacos, South Carolina ribs, steak, chicken, and many more. Salads with chicken, shrimp, or steak might be just what you want for lunch. There are also all kinds of burgers and sandwiches, imaginatively different sides, and desserts like the chocolate stack, tres leches cake, churros, or fruit sorbet. There are plenty of non-alcoholic beverages and beers, but don't forget the tequila selection.

Raglan Road Irish Pub and Restaurant

DDP: One credit (T) / Cost: $$ (TiW)
TYPE: Irish; Unique/Themed; Lunch and Dinner

Look for Raglan Road right next to Cookes of Dublin. In fact, they share a kitchen. This place is simply chockablock with cozy atmosphere. You could be forgiven for thinking you'd wandered into a delightful Dublin pub. There's even a song about Raglan Road recorded by the Dubliners, a group of Celtic singers:

> On Raglan Road on an Autumn Day,
> I saw her first and knew
> That her dark hair would weave a snare
> That I may one day rue...

Prices are slightly less expensive at lunch. Dinner starts at 3:00 p.m., and "pub grub" is served from 11:00 p.m. "until late." There's a dynamite Sunday brunch. Raglan Road Master Chef Kevin Dundon has created a brunch menu brimming with Irish treats, and the pub offers a selection of signature cocktails created especially for the Rollicking Raglan Brunch. Brunch guests can enjoy the chef's Full Irish Breakfast featuring sausage, black and white pudding, bacon, roasted tomato, mushrooms, and fried eggs with potato "roasties." More brunch options include a smoked salmon omelette and pancakes with crème fraiche, maple syrup, and berry compote. At noon the Raglan Road stage showcases Irish house bands and performances by the Raglan Road Dancers, "a troupe of pros who dazzle crowds with their colorful costumes, foot-stomping jigs and other fancy footwork." Come, tuck in, and make your next Sunday something special. Éirrin go Brách—Ireland forevermore!

Start with an Irish egg, mighty mussels, or smoked salmon with crème fraiche and capers. Appetizers to share include baby back ribs, pan-seared shrimp, Georges Bank scallops, and Dalkey duo (battered cocktail sausages and Dalkey mustard for dipping). Fresh salads like Go(at) Fig(ure), Cashel Castle, or SSS Beefy with creatively combined ingredients are a meal in themselves. Entrées run the gamut from a special shepherd's pie, lamb shank, and beef stew with Guinness, to burgers, seafood, heavenly ham, fried chicken, bangers (sausages), and lots more. Sides are unique and imaginative—garlic Parmesan truffle chips, crushed garden peas, smokey bacon, and almond-roasted Brussels sprouts are just a few of them.

Don't neglect the amazing desserts: fluffy lemon clouds (lemon and meringue), chocolate heaven, bread and butter pudding, Dundon's delight (raspberry Pavlova), trifle sinful, peach and apple crumble, and many more. It will be difficult to pick one, so pick several and share with the table or order the chef's dessert flight for yourself.

Raglan Road has you well covered with its drink menu. Bottled and draft beers (Guinness, naturally), non-alcoholic beverages, specialty libations (how about a Dublin donkey or a Baileys shake?), wines, and bubbly should perfectly accompany all that Irish deliciousness.

STK Orlando

DDP: One credit, lunch (T), Two cr., dinner (T) / Cost: $$-$$$$ (TiW)
TYPE: Steaks/Seafood; Fine/Signature; Lunch and Dinner

Anniversary, birthday, or just a fantastic dinner to remember—think STK. Your meal will be something very special. The venue is modern, sleek, and oh-so-chic. The food is fantastic. It's hard to go wrong with anything on the menu, but remember that such a beautiful meal will not come cheap. You'll pay *handsomely* for the privilege of dining here. A 28-ounce dry-aged porterhouse for two will set you back $97, but share it and celebrate! The menu isn't lengthy—it doesn't need to be. What's here is absolute perfection.

STK offers a dynamite weekend brunch that leaves few of your favorites behind. Share a "bag of stuffed donuts" or cinnamon monkey bread to start. Oysters on the half shell, hangover ceviché, Nueske's smoked bacon, tuna tartare or Wagyu beef sliders will go down easy. Try the beef short rib and egg sandwich for something substantial, or for lighter appetites there's avocado toast or the STK salad. Fried chicken and funnel cake, crab cakes Benedict, Old School (eggs, bacon, potatoes), lemon-ricotta pancakes, and lots of snazzy sides should provide energy for a big day or just relaxing around your resort's pool. Fabulous brunch cocktails suit the menu perfectly. The Perfect Bloody Mary, a mimosa, frosé (raspberry sorbet in a glass of chilled rosé), and a long list of others make it difficult to choose just one.

Dinner at STK is equally lavish. Salads and appetizers (try the wagyu burger called Lil' BRGs or order the shellfish platter for the table) are imaginative and luxurious. There's also a well-stocked raw bar. Entrées include chicken, lamb, seafood (smoked Maine lobster, Scottish salmon, seared tuna, and market fish), but the star of the show is steak. That whopping porterhouse, a petite filet mignon, sirloin, Delmonico, bone-in rib steak, bone-in filet, or dry-aged Delmonico will quell any carnivore's craving for red meat. Be perfectly specific when expressing your preference and expectation for doneness. Add truffle butter, a peppercorn crust, a couple of shrimp, or a lobster if you just can't get enough. Eight delightful sauces like STK, Bernáise, au poivre, blue butter, and four others will complement the meat beautifully. Sides are every bit as sinfully indulgent as the main courses. Think creamy Yukon potatoes, Parmesan truffle fries, sweet corn pudding, cucumbers and heirloom tomatoes, or lobster mac and cheese.

Not dessert, too? Well, if you *must*, there are many on hand to end your meal with something irresistible, but as I mentioned, there's no doubt that at STK, steak is the star.

The drink menu is as impressive as the food. Look for creative specialty cocktails (Cucumber Stilleto, ...Not Your Daddy's Manhattan, Naughty by Nature), a dozen lovely bottled beers, and a great many wonderful wines (mostly from California and France). Raise a glass of Moët & Chandon with your special someone and enjoy the evening!

Next, we'll explore eating options offered in the other two areas of Disney Springs, Town Center and West Side. While you won't encounter quite as many upscale restaurants, there are some unique eating venues to explore, like a Sprinkles Cupcake ATM for after-hours cravings, Bongos, AMC Movie Theatre Fork & Screen, Splitsville, and the Planet Hollywood Observatory. It's difficult to imagine that there are *more* dining choices yet to come, but dust off that imagination of yours because you're only halfway through the culinary cornucopia better known as Disney Springs.

Disney Springs, Part Two
Town Center and West Side

Town Center

Candy Cauldron

If you see someone walking around Disney Springs eating a "poisoned" apple that looks *exactly* like the one the Wicked Queen prepared for Snow White, don't be concerned. That's just one of the many kinds of candy and caramel apples you'll find at this sweet shop. Order one just the way you want it and then watch yours being made!

Amorette's Patisserie

DDP: No / Cost: $
TYPE: American. Quick Service; Snacks

Located next to Levi's and Volcom in Town Center, Amorette's is known for "sophisticated" snacks that you won't find just anywhere. These signature pastries are guaranteed to make your eyes light up, your tummy rumble, and your mouth water. They are as delectable as they are gorgeous, and their names are as fun as the treats themselves. 49th and Broadway/NY Cheesecake, Dancing with Pavlova/Light Meringue Crisp, Mickey Mousse, and Sunset on Mile Marker 0/Key Lime Tart will give you just a hint of what's on the menu.

The dome cakes are truly inspired. Order a Mickey, Minnie, Donald, Goofy, or Pluto. They're sure to make any dinner special! Call Amorette's at 407-934-3500 at least 72 hours in advance. Unfortunately, they won't deliver—you'll have to pick it up yourself at the bakery. You can choose small cakes or large. An eleven-layer red velvet and chocolate number filled with chocolate mousse and cherry mousse and frosted with Italian buttercream just amazes! The bakery has added three yummy sandwiches on focaccia and three kinds of crepes, so make a meal of your visit.

There's also an additional experience you may enjoy. Take a 90-minute class (coffee and other beverages included) to make your own Mickey cake for your family to praise (and then devour) later. Book online or call well in advance! It's $129, but the techniques you'll learn from the pros (how to pour glaçage and use edible paint) are priceless.

As you might imagine, there are lots of additional kinds of fancy pastries, beautiful to look at, and lots of champagne and sparkling wines to go with them. There's coffee and ganache hot chocolate, too. Amorette's, darling, where have you been all my life?

Blaze Fast Fire'd Pizza

DDP: No / Cost: $
TYPE: American; Quick Service; Snacks, Lunch, and Dinner

Fired pizza cooks quickly, and you can expect yours done in 180 seconds! The ingredients are artisanal while the dough is made from scratch. Choose original, higher rising, or gluten free dough to build your own pizza. The specialty pizzas are inventive and satisfying with just about every topping you can imagine. Get a simple salad to go with your pizza. Plenty of beers, wines, and non-alcoholic beverages are available at Blaze, and desserts, too. Try the s'more pie or other assorted sweets. It's a great place for a quick yet delicious meal or snack. Find it next to D-Luxe burger on the water that surrounds The Landing.

Coca-Cola Store Rooftop Beverage Bar

DDP: No / Cost: $
TYPE: American/Global; Quick Service; Drinks

Cokes, cocktails, alcoholic smoothies, and mocktails—they're all here waiting for you to try. You'll also find water, coffee, energy drinks, floats, icees, and icee floats. For an international treat, try the Cokes of the World tray or the combo tray.

You'll be surprised at how the rest of the world likes its Coca-Cola to taste. There's a "free-style experience" offering you five refills within an hour. There's no doubt about it—Coke is king here. Have a beverage and enjoy the panoramic view of Disney Springs from your rooftop vantage point. Things go better with Coke!

D-Luxe Burger

DDP: No / Cost: $
TYPE: American; Quick Service; Snacks, Lunch, and Dinner

It might look like a cute little farmhouse from the outside, but step inside and you'll find burgers galore. D-Luxe is located across from Blaze along the small water channel that surrounds The Landing and divides it from Town Center. Find classic, barbecue, El Diablo (chorizo, fried banana peppers, pepper jack cheese, chipotle mayo), a chicken "cluck" burger, and the veggie, with toppings and fresh-cut fries that come with free dipping sauces. Kids will enjoy ordering a "hamburger" red velvet macaroon for dessert that looks just like the big one. Get shakes or malts made with gelato, alcoholic or not, to go with that burger. There are plenty of Coke products, iced tea, and milk, as well as wines, draft beer, and hard cider plus three alcoholic sodas like ...Not your Father's Root Beer. You'll get a burger cooked to order, too, so tell 'em to make yours cooked the way *you* like it!

Häagen-Dazs

DDP: No / Cost: $
TYPE: American; Quick Service; Snacks

Hot, tired, and in need of a cool pick-me-up? Then look for this kiosk between YeSake and Wetzel's, right on the water. You can order a "dazzler" sundae like a banana split, mint chip, rocky road, or dulce split in small or regular sizes. There are sundaes in three sizes starting with "kiddie" and going up from there. Check out those shakes with toppings or without, and don't forget the frappes in coffee, mocha, and caramel. There are several ways to dress up your cone, so step up to the counter, decide on your favorite flavor, and place your order.

Joffrey's Smoothies

DDP: No / Cost: $
TYPE: American; Quick Service; Snacks

In addition to its Marketplace location, there's a Joffrey's Smoothies in Town Center as well, adjacent to YeSake and Wetzel's. As you've no doubt noticed, Joffrey's is found in many locales at Walt Disney World. The Purple Piñata , Flyin' Hawaiian, Mango Tango, Flamingo Frost, Razzy Jazzy, and several other concoctions are on the menu. This kiosk serves a tremendous variety of smoothies blended with Dippin' Dots vanilla yogurt and Minute Maid juice. Coffee with Kahlua, Baileys, or Jamesons, tea with vodka and lemon, and juices are also sold.

The Polite Pig

DDP: No / Cost: $$
TYPE: American Barbecue; Quick Service; Lunch and Dinner

Adjacent to the big water tower is a new arrival at Town Center, the latest restaurant venture of the Petrakis family. They already have two successful venues in the Orlando area, the Ravenous Pig and Cask & Larder. Expect to find locally sourced seasonal ingredients and a modern twist on traditional Southern barbecue. There's an open kitchen where you can see all the food preparation in action.

Snacks here are unusual. You'll find a hop salt pretzel with beer cheese fondue and IPA mustard, smoked wings, and a yummy slider trio that will leave you gasping. Find an eye-popping fifty kinds of bourbon available at the Bourbon Bar! There are a multitude of cocktails and beers on tap, too. Cobb or Caesar salads pair nicely with the barbecue selections. Sandwiches come with a pickle spear, but you may want to add one or more of the many appealing sides. Check out the brisket sandwich with pimento cheese, pickled jalapeños, and crispy onions. Baby back ribs, pork shoulder, brisket, and chicken are available "from the smoker," accompanied by slaw, Texas toast, and choice of one additional side like tomato and watermelon salad, crispy Brussels sprouts, roasted beets with smoked pecan granola, sweet potato tots, and lots more. Kids menu items are mini-ribs, mac and cheese, and chicken tenders. Orange blossom honey cake—a house specialty, carrot cake, or buttermilk chess pie are sure to sweeten the deal ... make that the *meal*.

Sprinkles Cupcakes

DDP: No / Cost: $
TYPE: American; Quick Service; Snacks

Located opposite Frontera Cocina on the water surrounding The Landing, you'll encounter "Cupcake Central." If you see a large crowd of excited and hungry guests milling around a glass door, you've very likely found Sprinkles Cupcakes. Famous Sprinkles is credited with starting the nation's cupcake craze, which, as you've no doubt discovered, is still going strong, especially here at Walt Disney World.

There are *four* kinds of red velvet cupcakes—regular, gluten-free, sugar-free, or vegan. With sixteen cupcake flavor options like chocolate marshmallow, salty caramel, or carrot, you're sure to find one, or *several*, that will suit you just perfectly. Ask about special and seasonal flavors, too. There are half a dozen cookie flavors, from traditional chocolate chip to salted oatmeal cornflake, and you'll also see a dozen regular (chocolate, vanilla, etc.) to wild (Cap'n Crunch) ice cream flavors to make the party complete. If you're being seriously decadent, order a cookie sandwich or a Sprinkles cupcake sandwich in your choice of flavors. There are brownie sundaes, cookie sundaes, triple scoops, and just about every sort of float, milkshake, or malt you can imagine. Beverages are also available, including tea, coffee, espresso, and latte.

If you get a Sprinkles craving and the shop is closed, there's an ATM cupcake machine that dispenses cupcakes for you 24/7. All the cupcakes are baked and frosted fresh every day. Use the easy touchscreen to select your flavor. Swipe your credit card (no cash). A robotic arm puts your choice into a little box and loads the dispenser which swivels open to reveal the treat. *Et voila*—instant Sprinkles!

Wetzel's Pretzels

DDP: No / Cost: $
TYPE: American; Quick Service; Snacks

Wetzel's is part of the cluster of snack kiosks at the far end of Town Center that includes YeSake, Häagen Dazs, and Joffrey's. Just as it is in the Marketplace, Wetzel's is a little stand where you can find delicious, fresh, warm pretzels. Get "sinful cinnamon" or "almond crunch," or try the baked cheese and pepperoni pretzel. For dipping, Wetzel's provides jalapeño or cheddar cheese, pizza, and sweet caramel sauce. If you're still hungry, order a hot dog or cheese dog with lemonade, frozen lemonade, or frozen granita.

YeSake

DDP: No / Cost: $
TYPE: Global; Quick Service; Snacks

The small, brick, stand-alone building near Wetzel's Pretzels holds a surprising amount of international goodies. World Flavors Tamaki (a Japanese wrap, but these *aren't* made with dried seaweed) gives you a tortilla wrapped around white rice and a main ingredient like ahi tuna, shrimp, yakiniku (it means grilled) beef, salmon and grilled chicken. Dress it up with add-ons such as shredded cheese, sour cream, aioli yuzu (Japanese citrus sauce), or avocado. If you've never tried a sake slush, this is your opportunity. There's a sake-rum, a sake-citrus tea slush, and sake-blue coconut frozen punch. Coke products and five kinds of canned beer are also on the menu. Quick food with an international twist makes a filling snack.

Frontera Cocina

DDP: One credit (T) / Cost: $$
TYPE: Mexican; Casual; Lunch and Dinner

Take the small bridge, the one just in front of Morimoto Asia, across the water and you'll find Frontera Cocina. If you've watched Chef Rick Bayless, six-time winner of the James Beard Foundation Award, on television, you'll know just what to expect here—fantastic, delicious, and authentic Mexican cuisine. Frontera means "border," but there is nothing borderline at this place. It's all simply fantastic. The restaurant from outside appears fairly standard, but the cuisine in this kitchen is a *big* cut above average, with a huge menu. If you have a favorite Mexican dish, you'll very likely be able to enjoy it here. Chef Rick didn't get where he is by playing it safe.

Sure, chips and salsa are available, but so is Sikal Pak, a creamy Yucatán pumpkin seed-habañero dip with crispy cucumber and jicama slices and warm tortilla chips. Tired of regular guacamole? Try the verde (green), bacon, or atomic version. Tortilla soup or queso fundito (melted cheese and chorizo) with warm corn tortilla are perfect starters. There are salads, tacos (try the succulent carne asada with soft tortillas), and tortas. Entrées include delectably prepared chicken, shrimp, carne asada (steak), carnitas (pork shoulder), and Oaxacan red chile chicken. Even the sides are a twist on the traditional. Yes, there is rice, but the rice comes studded with plantains and cilantro. You'll find beans, squash, Yukon potatoes, and more for sides. Desserts are a warm pecan pie bar, and a coconut lime quatro leches cake (right, *four* kinds of milk, not the standard three). The drink menu is as extensive as the food menu. Cocktails are plentiful: All the Pretty Girls, Mescal Moon, Barcelona Nights, plus plenty of others. Sparkling wines, an international wine list, beers galore, or a wide array of non-alcoholic beverages will help if you've had one too many habañero peppers! This is the perfect opportunity for you to enjoy real Mexican cuisine prepared beautifully, thoughtfully, and inventively! *Buen provecho.*

Frontera Cocina Quick Window

DDP: No / Cost: $
TYPE: Mexican; Quick Service; Snacks, Lunch, and Dinner

No time to stop for a full meal but still craving awesome Mexican food? Stop at the quick-service window and pick up some chips and guac with three tacos—either beef barbacoa (chipotle braised beef) or cochinita pibil (achiote braised pork shoulder). There are also margaritas, either a signature Frontera or a blood orange jalapeño. Beers and Coke products are available. If you like Mexican food, you can't go wrong at this spicy window.

West Side

AMC Theatre Fork & Screen

DDP: No / Cost: $-$$
TYPE: American; Casual; Lunch and Dinner

You will find this unusual theatre opposite the Planet Holly-wood Observatory. We're not just talking Milk Duds, popcorn, or Junior Mints here—not by a long shot. The theatre seats are comfy, and there's a counter or tray in front of them to hold your lunch or dinner. Wings, nachos, pretzel bites, tots, crispy Brussels sprouts, loaded wedge lettuce cups, or a sampler will get your started. There are some great sushi rolls, fries, three kinds of flatbreads, and many kinds of burgers are available, too. Bowls include teriyaki steak and rice, two kinds of chicken, mac and cheese, and gumbo mac, each loaded with enough goodies to make a complete meal. Caesar salad, chicken caesar wrap, Cobb salad, or chopped Cobb wraps are other choices. If the kids feel like chicken tenders, fish and chips, or quesadil-las, AMC has a substantial kids menu tailored just for younger tastes. Donuts with lots of dipping sauces, milkshakes, and "cake stacks" (cakes served in a Mason jar in flavors like straw-berry shortcake, birthday cake, and chocolate brownie) are sweet distractions. Still craving those Milk Duds? No worries. You can also order any of the traditional favorite movie candies, popcorn, Coke beverages, coffee, tea, and more to your heart's content. A full menu of alcoholic beverages is available, too, at MacGuffins Bar in the lobby. All you have to do is press a button to order your food. Going to the movies was *never* like this!

Fantasy Fare

DDP: No / Cost: $
TYPE: American; Quick Service; Snacks, Lunch, and Dinner

The bright red food truck carries good things to eat from the Magic Kingdom, and since it's on wheels, it moves around sometimes. You'll generally find it with the other food trucks next to the water between Bongos and Starbuck's. It's usually only open during dinner, except at very busy times when it's also open for lunch. You might find things like chicken and waffles, chicken strips, corn dogs, a swell shrimp-and-lobster mac and cheese. Coke beverages are available, too. Items on the menu will vary.

Italian Ice and Churros Stand

DDP: No / Cost: $
TYPE: Italian/Mexican; Quick Service; Snacks

There's another one of these, you'll remember, in the Marketplace. Four kinds of churros, lots of Italian ice flavors (order the "tye-dye" for something beautiful *and* refreshing), gelato in several flavors, plus soft serve ice cream in cones, waffle cones, and cups are served here. Get Coke products and Powerade, too.

Springs' Street Tacos

DDP: No / Cost: $
TYPE: Mexican; Quick Service; Snacks

The newest kid on the food truck block is this beautifully and brightly decorated venue where you'll find five kinds of tacos, chips with salsa or guac, plus a combo meal. (The truck was formerly called Namaste Café with foods from the Animal Kingdom, so don't bother looking for that one.) You'll feel like you're suddenly south of the border when you bite into a grilled steak (carne asada), chicken adobo, grilled fish (mahi with pumpkin seed butter), or crispy pork belly taco. Tacos come with queso fresco, cilantro, and lime, just like they do in Mexico. Vegetarians aren't forgotten: there's a rice and beans version, too. Olé!

Starbucks

DDP: No / Cost: $
TYPE: American; Quick Service; Snacks

Starbuck's favorites like frappuchino, espresso, latte, smoothie, iced coffee, tea, refreshers, or hot chocolate are on the menu at this walk-up counter in sizes grande (16 oz.), venti (24 oz.), or trenta (30 oz.). Try adding a flavor or a shot of espresso.

World Showcase of Flavors

DDP: No / Cost: $
TYPE: Global; Quick Service; Snacks

Like the other two food trucks, this one is mobile and usually open only at dinnertime. It features items from the Epcot

International Food and Wine Festival. Menu selections will vary, but you can expect to find choices like Chilean Steak, pork belly, chicken demitasse, or meatball pomodoro sandwiches. Coke beverages and wine are available.

Bongos Cuban Café

DDP: One credit (T) / Cost: $$
TYPE: Cuban; Casual; Lunch and Dinner

Gloria Estefan is the visionary behind Bongos, a café that recreates the vibe of Havana, Cuba, in the 1950s. It's right on the water. Bar stools are giant, colorful conga drums. Bamboo lines the walls and bright glass light fixtures add to the festive ambience here. Enormous potted palms and plants bring the tropics indoors.

Soups and salads are available with classic Cuban garlic toast. Appetizers are hearty, spicy, and delicious. The Estefan Cuban Combo serves two and might be the way to go if you're not sure what to pick. Crispy pork bites, ham croquettes, fried calamari, loaded baked potatoes, bacon-wrapped plantains (maduros), Cuban empanadas, black bean hummus, and many more will start off your taste of Cuba meal with flair. Beef nine savory ways, pork, ribs, chicken, and seafood should please just about everyone in your group. There's also a helpful section called the "Calorie Conscious Cuban" for those watching their waistlines. Those items are gluten-free and grilled. Traditional Latin desserts like flan, rice pudding, churros, and tres leches cake are joined on the dessert menu by chocolate mousse, chocolate lava cake, and guava New York-style cheesecake. To quench your thirst, you'll discover a lovely array of inventive cocktails, wines from California and South America, and plenty of beers. Many non-alcoholic choices are available, too.

The lively décor is almost as great as the cuisine at Bongos.

Bongos Cuban Café Express

DDP: No / Cost: $
TYPE: Cuban; Quick Service; Snacks, Lunch, and Dinner

Several of the menu items at Bongos can be found here, too, and it's right next door. Portions are smaller, so you could try a couple of different items and share among the group. The

Cuban Party Box includes a ham croquette, potato stuffed with beef, a mini Cuban sandwich, and a guava pastry for dessert. The Cuban sandwich made from slow-roasted pork, Swiss, pickles, and mustard is a sure-fire winner. Soups, salads, appetizers, and wraps make a great, quick meal or snack. There are entrées as well, but no substitutions: chicken bites, beef bites, and minced beef. Side orders like plantain chips, sweet plantains, or black beans can be added to your order. Plenty of children's items are also on the menu. Desserts are chocolate chip cookies, flan, cheese pastry, or guava pastry. Coffee, tea, fountain beverages, beers and wines, and more will go well with any of the Cuban food at Bongos. *Muy delicioso.*

House of Blues Restaurant and Bar
DDP: One credit (T) / Cost: $$ (TiW)
TYPE: Southern/American/Global; Casual; Lunch and Dinner

Located next to the big water tower, the cuisine at House of Blues is Southern and global, and the music is cool—and there are a lot more styles than just the blues. You might hear R and B, hip hop, reggae, or something entirely different. Fantastic regional and national bands play here while you dine in style. There's a popular Happy Hour every day.

The Sunday brunch is scheduled occasionally, so check for dates before you come. It is an all-you-care-to-enjoy meal, with gospel performers who will sing out the "good news." It's loud and down-home style, so don't expect to carry on a quiet conversation. You can expect the usual breakfast items like pastries, eggs, ham, sausage, eggs, made-to-order omelettes, and biscuits and gravy, but there is also Creole chicken jambalaya, smoked BBQ chicken, carving stations, chicken and waffles, and other special items like white chocolate banana bread pudding with crème anglaise.

Lunch and dinner menus are the same. Start with hand-stretched, grilled flatbreads, each using fresh, inventive combinations of ingredients. Appetizers range from traditional Southern, like corn bread with maple butter and pulled pork sliders, to currently trendy, like voodoo shrimp and spicy fried calamari. There's a "steamin' tot mess" you may find appealing. American classics abound: St. Louis-style ribs, Cajun chicken, jambalaya, shrimp and grits, buttermilk fried chicken, meatloaf, salmon, steak, and lots more. There are build-your-own burgers and signature sandwiches, and don't forget the many varieties of salads and sides such as house-made coleslaw, BBQ beans, sweet potato fries, and mac and cheese. The bourbon bread pudding is jaw-dropping. Key lime pie, cheesecake, and chocolate mousse are on the dessert menu as well. Kids will find plenty to make them smile on their special menu. There is a greater than usual variety of non-alcoholic specialty beverages and Coke products, coffee, and tea. Sparkling wines, red and white, and a large listing of beers and hard cider are served.

House of Blues, The Smokehouse

DDP: No / Cost: $
TYPE: American; Quick Service; Snacks, Lunch, and Dinner

A little building in front of the House of Blues specializes in smoked meats. For a quick meal or snack, it's a satisfying option. You'll find slow-smoked brisket on a brioche bun with coleslaw, St. Louis-style ribs, pulled pork, pulled chicken, smoked turkey legs, hot dogs, and a huge platter of Smokehouse nachos to which you can add meat(s) of your choice. Sides go well with the main dishes: coleslaw, beans, or chips. A kids menu is available with an all-beef hot dog or a pulled pork slider. Sweets are stocked here, along with Coke beverages, juices, wine, and beer.

Planet Hollywood Observatory

DDP: One credit (T) / Cost: $$ (TiW)
TYPE: American;Casual; Lunch and Dinner

Planet Hollywood, the franchise that began in 1991 as an answer to the Hard Rock Café's wild popularity, just underwent a Hollywood-style face lift in Orlando, reopening in January 2017. The globe has morphed into an observatory dome with outside balcony seating at Stargazer Lounge. You'll find twenty craft beers on tap and ten signature cocktails. Four dining levels inside have a view of the 4,500 square-foot video wall with projections that look absolutely real, due to a high-def, three dimensional visual effect. An interesting museum's worth of Hollywood memorabilia is displayed inside.

The menu has lots of popular items with some new names plus some delightful newcomers, like chicken crunch, five cheese dip, hummus trio, and a "cosmic sampler" to start. Salads are spinach and berries, chicken Caesar, Hollywood Bowl (turkey, bacon, Swiss, hard boiled egg, cheese, and more), and steak salad. Four great pastas join a crowd of "big bite burgers" (including a lean turkey burger or—on the opposite end of the caloric spectrum—one topped with bacon and mac-and-cheese) and "knuckle sandwiches." Try the house-roasted turkey, Swiss, cranberry sauce, BBQ chips, LTOP (lettuce, tomatoes, onions, pickles), and "donkey sauce" (chef Guy Fieri's concoction of mayo, garlic, Worcester, and mustard; Fieri, in fact, created the burger and sandwich menu here) on a garlic-buttered pretzel roll called the Pic-A-Nik. Entrées range from steaks, ribs, and chicken, to salmon and lobster. Add a side salad or a whole, broiled lobster to create your own surf-and-turf combo. Sides are what you'd expect, but the addition of freshly cut fruit is a nice change. Healthy choices are possible here, but you have to look closely to find them.

Single-serving desserts are as expected, except for the different and fab British sticky toffee pudding, but there are some eye-popping shareable sweet treats like the Planet Meltdown or an asteroid-sized Brownie Sundae Martini. Drinks includes shakes (with starry names) galore, many appealing non-alcoholic specialty drinks, and a wide assortment of wines, hard cider, and beers. Check out the three specialty beverages for children if you have them in your party. The drinks come with signature cups, adorable names, and appealing ingredients. Kids will have no trouble choosing from their own menu (spaghetti, mac and cheese, cheese pizza, and chicken tenders with a special dessert of the day) and there's so much to see here that they'll be kept busy watching all the action, which includes some live entertainment.

Splitsville Dining Room

DDP: One credit (T) / Cost: $-$$ (TiW)
TYPE: American; Casual; Lunch and Dinner

Eating in a bowling alley was never like this! The luxury lanes and upscale modern décor make this an entirely different experience. It's 50,000 square feet filled with bowl-ing, billiards, bars, and dining—plus live entertainment. As they say in their advertising literature, "Not your typical bowl-ing alley menu. Hope you don't mind." Oh, you *won't*.

Appetizers are sure to please most. Macho nachos, filet slid-ers, Parmesan chicken tenders, dynamite shrimp, ahi tuna and avocado, and more will start off your meal with a strike. Sushi rolls such as California, California crunch, ninja crunch, super tuna, crouching tiger, and volcano roll are a pleasant change of pace. There are pizzas in all your favorite flavors: margherita, meat lovers, veggie, firehouse, Hawaiian, and gluten free, to name a few. Bowls with an Asian flair come next, followed by burgers and sandwiches. All that and we haven't even touched on the entrées. You'll find main courses like pulled pork, mahi mahi and voodoo shrimp, steak, chicken Alfredo, salmon, and fish and chips. Splitsville also serves entrée salads with chicken, ahi tuna, or turkey.

As you'd expect, desserts here are equally fun. Try a Ghirar-delli brownie with ice cream, an ice-cream sundae, a cupcake, float, or a "giant cake" with layers stacked so tall that "you just might need a ladder," patrons are jokingly advised. There is an extensive list of frozen cocktails, bowl drinks to share, classic cocktails, draft and bottled beers, red and white wines, and non-alcoholic beverages. Younger guests in your party will appreciate the kid-pleasing children's menu.

This is an inspired way to mix games and goodies in Disney Springs, with choices to spare!

Wolfgang Puck Express

DDP: One credit (S) / $
TYPE: American/Californian; Quick Service; Breakfast, Lunch, Dinner

Wolfgang Puck Grand Café and The Dining Room at Wolfgang Puck are closed while undergoing a major refurbishment. The restaurant is slated to reopen as Wolfgang Puck's Bar and Grill with plans to "revolutionize the traditional bar and grill concept". For a fast yet fresh and flavorful breakfast, lunch or dinner, stop here for hearty breakfast pizza, omelet, Belgian waffle, or that crave-worthy corn flake French toast. For later in the day, soups, pizzas (of course!), and classic entrées like a bacon-wrapped meatloaf sandwich, rotisserie chicken, and mac and cheese are all great picks. Many kinds of salads, wraps, and sandwiches are available for you to grab and go. While the main restaurant is closed, the menu at the Express has expanded considerably. You can order oven-roasted salmon, bacon-wrapped meatloaf, or half a rotisserie chicken. Frozen yogurt and a fresh fruit cup are health-conscious options, but you can also find crème brûlée with berries or vanilla bean cheesecake. It's a fun place with bright décor and an even brighter menu.

Disney Springs is always growing and changing, and 2018 will see the addition of Wolfgang Puck's latest bar and grill concept and Jaleo, a new Spanish restaurant courtesy of Chef José Andrés. Jaleo will "feature an extensive menu of tapas that reflects the rich regional diversity of traditional and contemporary Spanish cuisine" like the famous saffron rice and seafood paella and jamón (ham) Iberico de Bellota. The Edison, announced in 2015, has yet to open. Its style will be a fusion of industrial (a 1920s Los Angeles electric plant) and gothic "with a nod to old world sophistication and romance." Okay, if you say so, Disney Springs. Chef Tony Mantuano is opening a restaurant in the old Portobello space with a new name, décor, and Italian menu.

At Disney Springs you have to carefully evaluate your preferences. Do you like loud and lively? Try House of Blues, Planet Hollywood Observatory, AMC Fork and Screen, or Splitsville. Something quick to hold you and the gang for a while? Think about the food trucks and quick-service windows like Bongos, Frontera, Morimoto Street, or Wolfgang Puck Express. Morimoto Asia, STK Orlando, or the BOATHOUSE will give you an incredible meal worth remembering. Want a place you probably won't find back at home? How about T-Rex Café, Raglan Road, or Jock Lindsey's Hangar Bar? For a special celebration, order something sweet and lovely from Amorette's, and Sprinkles ATM will see you though a midnight cupcake craving. Your choices are as varied as the many guests at Walt Disney World. The culinary world awaits you at Disney Springs. Dive in!

Unique and Signature Dining

The Best of the Disney Resort Hotels

All of the Disney resort hotels have on-site restaurants and places to buy snacks. A handful of the dining establishments located at the resort hotels, however, are truly exceptional. They offer special unique/themed experiences and fine/signature dining fare that measure up with the best anywhere on Disney property—or anywhere else, for that matter. Regardless of where you might be staying, you can take advantage of eating at any of the following restaurants, but many if not most will require advanced dining reservations if you hope to get a table. I've said this before, but it is well worth repeating:

> Even with an ADR, you *don't* have a table waiting for you at, say, 8:00 p.m. Rather, you have a *reservation for the next available table that opens up after you arrive* at 8:00 p.m. This simple fact eludes a large number of guests who vociferously complain that "their" table wasn't available on time.

There aren't many fine dining establishments in the country that follow Disney's unusual reservation policy, so people should be forgiven for being upset when they show up for a table they reserved six months in advance and then must wait for up to an hour to be seated, or even longer. It doesn't happen all the time, but it does happen sometimes. Be forewarned.

Be aware that prices and menus change frequently without notice. The entries in this guide will give you a good idea of what *kinds* of foods you may expect at a particular restaurant. Specific menu items are not guaranteed.

Guests occasionally report being poorly treated by a member of the wait staff, even at some of these luxury dining establishments. Should this happen to you, don't hesitate to discreetly bring it to the attention of the maître d'hôtel who should be able to rectify the situation immediately. Do not accept poor service or rudeness. There is no need to get into a protracted battle of wills with the wait staff. Neither should you suffer or seethe in silence and later post a scathing indictment of the entire restaurant. Be polite, be friendly, but be firm. *When you are paying handsomely for excellent food and service, you have every right to expect it.*

Meals at these places are not bargains. Eating at *any* of them is a moderate to major financial splurge; eating at one certainly won't be easy on your wallet, so don't expect to find any "good deals" here. If you have something special to celebrate or simply feel like indulging in a memorable meal, then consider the following restaurants, which are listed in alphabetical order by the name of the hotel where they are located.

Note: Some of the resort restaurants feature character buffets. Those are covered in the next chapter.

Animal Kingdom Lodge

Boma—Flavors of Africa

DDP: One credit (T) /Cost: $$ (TiW)
TYPE: African; Unique/Themed; Breakfast and Dinner

Just about everyone will find many offerings to their liking at this family-friendly buffet that looks like nothing so much as an open-air African marketplace. Even the carving stations are positioned under thatched roofs. Menu items are on a "rotation," so don't expect to find every one at every meal. Breakfast entrées include all the usual American standards (pancakes, waffles, eggs, ham, oatmeal, French toast bread pudding, and more) in addition to some African additions like sweet plantains and an African fruit fool (a mix of fruit and custard). Try the Kenyan press coffee to accompany your breakfast buffet, but you'll find other beverages of every sort, too.

The dinner buffet is equally pleasing. A tremendous array of soups and salads, many you'll recognize and others more exotic, are on attractive display. Entrées include salmon, pork, chicken, fish, or beef, along with African pap (porridge made from softly ground maize), fufu (sometimes made with green plantain flour and cassava), and boboti (minced meat and an egg-based topping) to liven things up a bit. The same variety applies to the side dishes. Yes, there are familiar mashed and sweet potatoes, but there is also peanut rice, Zulu cabbage, and geel rys—the name means yellow rice, and it often accompanies boboti. As is usual at Disney buffets, desserts are plentiful and appealing: key lime cheesecake, a pretty zebra dome, apple cobbler, and a Kenyan coffee tart are just a few of them. The setting is exotic, and so is the food—but not so exotic that everyone in the party can't find something delicious at Boma. It's a good value; feel free to have "all you care to enjoy" here.

Jiko—The Cooking Place

DDP: Two credits (T) / Cost: $$$-$$$$ (TiW)
TYPE: Indian/Mediterranean/African; Fine/Signature; Dinner

The décor is beautiful with a wall that changes colors like the sunset. What appear to be birds in flight are suspended overhead. Window seats have a pretty view of the "savanna." Banquette seats are extremely close together. The food here is not for everyone. Jiko is more adventurous and different than typical Disney dining establishments. Appetizers include grilled wild boar tenderloin, Jiko salad (Land Pavillion greens, stone fruit, pistachio halva, grilled Halloumi cheese, apricot-ginger dressing), manti dumplings with mint chutney, corn soup (with pork shoulder, poached egg, lemon-curd corn) or heirloom tomatoes. There is an artisanal cheese selection, none of which have anything to do with Africa. They come, instead, from Utah, Vermont, and the Canadian border. Descriptions of the cheeses are quite specific:

> Bayley Hazen Blue—This natural-rind blue cheese is named for the iconic Bayley Hazen Military Road that traverses the Northeast Corridor of the US and Canada. The usual peppery spice character associated with traditionally produced blue cheese takes a backseat to sweet, nutty, and grassy flavors. The breakdown of fats and proteins during ripening often show a distinct liquorice (sic) flavor.

Menu items from "the cooking place" are sometimes cryptic. What, you might be excused for wondering, are "inguday tibs in brik" or "manti dumplings." Don't fret. Everything including the ingredients is described. Entrées are equally eclectic and mix the usual with the very unusual. You'll find filet mignon, chicken, lamb, fish, and beef short ribs alongside Durham Ranch (based in Reno, Nevada) elk loin or vegetarian West African Kori corn. Enhancements are coconut-curry shrimp, lobster tail, and Egyptian kushari (ancient grains, etc.). Desserts include Kilimanjaro Safari Sunset, granadilla melktert, and malva pudding (luckily, the ingredients are listed; unluckily, the ingredients are sometimes even more indecipherable than the names of the desserts themselves). Everything is costly. Mickey Check meals are pan-seared fish, and grilled chicken. Several more kids meals are offered as well. There are a great many specialty teas on the menu, some unusual after-dinner coffee drinks, a couple of South African wines, many brandies, ports, single malt whiskies, and liqueurs. Few non-alcoholic beverages are offered, so don't expect fountain beverages.

Guest reviews sometimes harshly criticize the service at Jiko and other times praise it to the skies. That's true of almost any restaurant, but here the quality of the service would seem to be more uneven than at most of the other fine/signature-dining venues. It is never necessary to accept poor service at a Disney restaurant. Make your concerns known, clearly, politely, and promptly to your maître d'hôtel.

Saana

DDP: One credit (T) / Cost: $$ (TiW)
TYPE: African/Indian; Unique/Themed; Breakfast Lunch, Dinner

Saana is beautiful. Attention to detail makes dining here a treat. The colors are vibrant and cheerful. Look through the large picture windows to see African animals browsing just outside. Breakfast provides a wide assortment of the unusual and the familiar. Yogurt parfait, Boerewors pie, fruit plate, fruit sosatie, Boere breakfast, Safari waffle—see what I mean? Add whole fruit, assorted pastries and everyone should be set. The Indian-style bread sampler is a popular starter with five types of bread and three choices of dipping sauces. Soups (including oxtail at dinner only), lamb kefta skewers, seasonal soup, Boere-wors (South African sausage) and spiced eggs, a salad sampler, and shrimp round out the appetizers. The menu offers Tandoori chicken or shrimp and several appealing sandwiches and burgers. At dinner, lamb, steak, duck, fish, and the highly regarded butter chicken with basmati rice are just some of the entrées. Finish with puddings, tarts, African triple mousse (three kinds of chocolate mousse), caramel ndizi, or a Spice Trade candy bar. Sanaa has wide appeal, good value for your money, lovely atmosphere, and not-your-average park food.

BoardWalk Resort

Flying Fish
DDP: Two credits (T) / Cost: $$$-$$$$ (TiW)
TYPE: Seafood/American; Fine/Signature; Dinner

A table at Flying Fish is *the* hot ticket on the BoardWalk these days. Call at the earliest possible moment if you hope to eat here. Reservations are extremely difficult to obtain. A dress code is in effect (and enforced).

Prices are steep (Maine Lobster Nero Pasta will set you back $58) but, judging from Flying Fish's popularity, many people think it's worth the price for a true gastronomic splurge. You can watch your food being prepared on the kitchen stage. The appetizers are Canadian blue mussels, mango-crusted grouper cheeks, "The Evolution of Cheese," Mile Zero shrimp cocktail, and Kurobuta pork belly. The freshest of seafood is the star of the show. Salmon, Hokkaido scallops, Spanish octopus/cobia/Key West pink shrimp, and wild Alaskan halibut are joined on the menu by free-range chicken, Wagyu strip loin, and a veal chop. Desserts are unusual and exciting. Try Under the Sea or Florida Reef for some surprisingly delicious, masterful flavor combinations. All of the desserts are uniquely different from what you'll find elsewhere, so save room! The kids aren't forgotten. Three Mickey Check meals are supplemented with flying fish and chips, corn-battered rock shrimp, or grilled beef strip loin. Kids can order free-range chicken noodle soup or fruit as an appetizer. The specialty cocktails and coffees are befitting of this heady culinary experience. The French press coffee pot for two would go nicely with any of the phenomenal desserts. Sommelier wine selections are international and thoughtfully chosen to complement the food. You won't go wrong dining at Flying Fish—*if* you can get a reservation.

Contemporary Resort

California Grill

DDP: Two credits (T) / Cost: $$$-$$$$ (TiW)
TYPE: American/Seafood/Sushi; Fine/Signature; Brunch and Dinner

The Contemporary is one of the two original Walt Disney World hotels. It opened in 1971 and is still, after some refurbishment, going strong. The monorail runs right through the lobby on an elevated track. Dining here is every bit as gorgeous as you'd expect, and the view of the Magic Kingdom's Happily Ever After fireworks display is fantastic. During daylight, twilight, or at night, vistas of the Seven Seas Lagoon are gorgeous. In large part, this is what sets the California Grill above other restaurants—the view. The food is good *and* costly. Service varies. Some guests on the Disney Dining Plan report shabby treatment. Not every meal is going to be superlative, but the wait staff here has been condescending, even rude, at times, which is never a pleasant experience. You shouldn't accept that at any time, but especially not at a Disney resort hotel.

Brunch includes several items presented to the table. A selection of baked goods, cocktails for the adults and a non-alcoholic "sparkling Mimosa" for the children, plus coffee come out out first. Then, you serve yourself from a buffet. Selections are not the same as you'll find at most Disney brunches. California rolls, shrimp tempura, house-made charcuterie, Andrea's Pear Salad (a personal favorite—tiny reds and greens, pear, young goat's milk cheese, candied pecans, and a vanilla-golden raisin vinaigrette), spicy tuna tekka maki rolls, hardwood smoked salmon, house-made charcuterie, and more are on the menu. Entrées aren't usual, either, and include U-10 shrimp, the chef's omelette selection, grilled hanger steak, eggs Benedict, and blueberry pancakes. For dessert, try either "small minis," macaroons, or chocolate truffles. You may also order featured wines by the glass, and cocktails.

Many people try to schedule their dinner around the nightly fireworks at Magic Kingdom, which occurs pretty late during the summer months. That can lead to frustration. It's difficult to "fine tune" exactly when your table will actually be available. If you've eaten here earlier in the evening, however, just hold on to your receipt. Bring it back before the fireworks, and show it to be admitted to the outdoor viewing deck.

Dinner at the California Grill can be a great meal. It can also be so-so or sub-par, especially if your steak is sent out virtually raw when you ordered medium. Lots of problems can be avoided if you are as specific as possible about your preferences regarding exactly the way you'd like your food prepared.

Start with cheesesteak or BLT flatbread or "oysters Rockefeller revisited." There is a wide selection of charcuterie, including wild boar belly pancetta, venison terrine, and duck liver pâté. Sushi rolls and sashimi are offered in common and uncommon varieties. The soups, salads, and appetizers are mouthwatering. A creamy Brentwood corn bisque with Maine lobster, handcrafted charcuterie, Sonoma goat cheese ravioli, California peach salad, artisanal cheese, and heirloom tomato salad ought to whet your appetite. Entrées include wild halibut from Alaska, Kurobuta park rib chop, Angus filet, line-caught black grouper, pork tenderloin, and the irresistibly upscale take on ramen: shave Wagyu and shrimp ramen with enoki mushroom, bok choy, corn, and ajitsuke egg (soft boiled and marinated) in fragrant broth. Cheeses, fruit-based desserts, California beignets, no-sugar banana cake, and a warm chocolate pudding cake bring your meal to an end. Mickey Check meals are beef tenderloin, chicken, and wild salmon. Kids can also order cheese pizza or mac and cheese. Some nice Napa wines are available by the glass. Some of the cocktails have clever California names like the Monte Ray, Anaheim Mule, and Napa Blue Martini (the olives are stuffed with blue cheese). Classic beers and ciders are well represented and come from Ireland, California, Michigan, Florida, Scotland, Belgium, Colorado, Sweden and New York.

Come for the view, but stay for the food.

The Wave...of American Flavors

DDP: One credit (T) / Cost: $-$$ (TiW)
TYPE: American; Unique/Themed; Breakfast (Buffet), Lunch, Dinner

What a funny name, ellipsis periods and all, but the emphasis is on good, healthful foods. The entrance is lit with blue and is meant to evoke diving into the tube of a breaking wave. The light fixtures inside look like jellyfish, and the wave motif is carried out in the ceiling and the backs of the chairs.

Breakfast is an all-you-care-to-enjoy buffet and is a reasonable value for the money. It includes all the favorite standbys. In addition, there's also an egg-white frittata, citrus-scented French toast, the Continental, eggs Benedict, or signature sweet potato pancakes. Lunch and dinner are non-buffet. Lunch has soups, salads, PEI mussels, and crab cakes for appetizers, and sandwiches, salads, and burgers, with some sweetly different desserts like a trio of seasonal sweets and a flight of petite chocolate desserts. Dinner appetizers feature bacon and eggs and PEI mussels, along with soups and salads. There are plenty of choices. Entrées include steak, fish, pork chop, cioppino, noodle bowl, wild salmon, scallops, chicken, and potato gnocchi. Desserts include artisanal cheeses, a trio of sorbet flavors, and no-sugar crème brûlée with berries. Mickey Check meals are fish, chicken, penne, or pork. There are loads of non-alcoholic beverages, in addition to organic draft beers, and cocktails. The prices are fairly reasonable, especially when compared with other places on this list, the service ranks highly, and the food is at least average or above.

Coronado Springs Resort

Maya Grill

DDP: One credit (T) / Cost: $-$$ (TiW)
TYPE: Mexican/American; Unique/Themed; Dinner

With echoes of Mayan temples and paintings surrounding you, you'll dine in the style of Old Mexico, but the cuisine is definitely Nuevo Latino. Appetizers are inventive. You'll find the popular queso fundito (melted cheese topped with chorizo/sausage and served with tortillas), tacos Durango, Acapulco roasted beet salad, and many others equally appealing. Steaks, red snapper, veggie tacos, shrimp tacos, fajitas, chicken, pork, and short ribs are spicy but friendly to American palates. Several seasonal signature dishes, higher in price, are available. Desserts are typical south-of-the-border favorites like flan and fruit sorbet. Non-alcoholic beverages as well as a huge variety of international wines and margaritas are available. Maya Grill is perfect if you're looking for something out of the ordinary.

Grand Floridian Resort & Spa

Victoria & Albert's
DDP: No / Cost: $$$-$$$$
TYPE: Modern/American; Fine/Signature; Dinner

The V&A dining experience is *not* for everyone. Are dining plans accepted? No, and it is extremely expensive. No one under ten is admitted. It's not at all unusual for a couple to pay as much as $1,000 for their dinner, including tax and gratuity. It's also not unusual for a multi-course dinner to last three-and-a-half to four-and-a-half hours. Many rave about the place and claim, perhaps to rationalize that kind of financial outlay for a single meal, that it is "worth every penny." For that kind of money, people tend to expect the very finest food and service, but it's impossible to meet *everyone's* lofty expectations. Yes, of course, the strictest Disney dress code applies here. Don't worry if the gentleman has no sport coat, as they have many on hand to lend. For some, the stuffy atmosphere is off-putting. For others, the lengthy description and discussion about the food is inappropriately detailed and intrusive, even unintentionally humorous. If money is no object and you can manage to lower your expectations to a reasonable level, you might very well enjoy a meal here. If not, you'd be wise to dine elsewhere.

First course is amuse bouche, literally something to amuse the mouth; second course is caviar ($210 for one oz.), hearts of palm and shrimp, or seared tuna with mango and avocado; third course is turbot, a scallop, or bass; fourth course is duck with "turnip kraut" or pork, fifth course is Australian Kobe-style beef, lamb, veal with mushroom lasagne, or Miyazaki beef; sixth course is a selection of cheese or chocolate gelato;

seventh course is chocolate mousse, banana cake, Grand Marnier soufflé, chocolate soufflé, or green apple mousse. Last comes coffee. It will cost about $200 for the seven-course meal and another $95 for wine pairings, *not* including tax and gratuity. The menu changes seasonally, so this list gives you an idea of the kinds of things you might expect to find on the menu.

There are fourteen tables in the Dining Room, but only four in Queen Victoria's Room (in a setting so intimate that some diners report feeling like they're eating in someone else's house, someone they don't actually know—a bit under the microscope, in other words). Every table is assigned two waiters. If dining in the kitchen and interacting with the chef sounds like something you'd enjoy, book the Chef's Table ten-course meal. There is only one seating for it per night. As many as ten or as few as two people may make a reservation. At press time, prices for dinner at the Chef's Table begin at $250 with wine pairings adding another $150, and that doesn't include tax or gratuity.

The V & A is a sixteen-year recipient of the AAA Five Diamond award. As long as you know *exactly* what you're signing on for ahead of time, you should enjoy your special evening here.

Cítricos

DDP: Two credits (T) / Cost: $$$ (TiW)
TYPE: Mediterranean/American; Fine/Signature; Dinner

Cítricos is elegant and comfortable with a welcoming air. The focus is on high-quality fine dining. Children (they should be well-behaved and you ought to dine with them on the early side) will be very well taken care of by the friendly staff. Once, in desperation, I asked for a banana for my hungry grandson from a fabulous fresh fruit display, and it was immediately presented to him without question.

Start with charcuterie—it's delicious—or try a Cítricos cheese board. The cheese course has a nice selection of four cheeses. The first course has many options: crab salad, Key West shrimp and baby spinach, beet salad, flatbread, and more. Entrées are beef short ribs, chicken, steaks, seafoods, and vegetarian options. Potatoes, crispy Brussels sprouts, mushrooms, and scallops are the enhancements. Desserts are equally appealing. Tiramisù, Florida key lime pie, warm choc-olate-banana torte, lemon-scented cheesecake, fruit sorbet, and other delectables will please just about anyone. Mickey Check meals are shrimp, beef, chicken, and pasta. Children can also choose from steak, pepperoni pizza, shrimp, mac and cheese, chicken, or macaroni with meat sauce. A large number of attractive specialty cocktails grace the menu, along with four international wines and a great many beers.

Like Narcoossee's, Cítricos is a beautifully appointed dining location. If you have any issues, the perfectly charm-ing maître d'hôtel (trained on the Disney *Magic* cruise ship) will gladly and promptly rectify them. Cítricos is a perfect place to celebrate that special occasion or simply to enjoy a very pleasant meal.

Narcoosee's

DDP: Two credits (T) / Cost: $$-$$$ (TiW)
TYPE: Seafood/American; Fine/Signature; Sunday Brunch and Dinner

The interior of Narcooseess's is lovely (and a little less formal than Cítricos) with a wrap-around view of the Seven Seas Lagoon. There is a dress code, but it is "business casual" (and much less stuffy than the one imposed at Victoria & Albert's): "Men may wear slacks, jeans or dress shorts and collared shirts. Jackets are optional. Women may wear dresses, skirts or dress shorts with blouses or sweaters. Not permitted in the dining room are tank tops, swimsuits, swimsuit cover-ups, hats for gentlemen, cut-offs, torn clothing and shirts with offensive language or graphics."

The unusual name is derived from the Creek word for "little bear." Brunch means specialty drinks for everyone and a pastry basket for the table. Appetizers include soup, salad, cheeses, and salmon. Entrées are brioche French toast, chicken and waffles, halibut, lobster eggs Benedict (you read that correctly), steak and eggs, an omelette your way, line-caught swordfish, or croque madame. A "trio" of desserts is served.

Dinner at Narcoossee's offers a selection of delicious soups and salads. Try the surprising watermelon and tomato Caprese with burrata cheese and pistachio or perhaps the decadent butter-poached Maine lobster bisque. Appetizers like PEI

mussels, shrimp and grits, calamari, cheeses, or poached and chilled shrimp will start your meal off beautifully. Entrées are varied and appealing. Steak, lobster, grouper, swordfish, chicken, pork, scallops, shrimp, and Cheshire pork rib chop with fruit chutney give most people something they will like. Those all-too-addictive "enhancements" are asparagus, potatoes, roasted Brussels sprouts, and a heavenly sauce béarnaise (for that grass-fed filet mignon entrée you just couldn't resist). Cheesecake, sorbet, sugarless chocolate torte, apple tart, crème brûlée, and other desserts will finish off a delicious dinner. Mickey Check meals are chicken, veggie burger, shrimp, or pasta. Kids meals are steak, mac and cheese, chicken tenders, or a burger. Some attractive Napa wines and specialty coffee drinks are served.

Narcoosee's is a gorgeous place to dine with lovely scenery and expansive views of the lagoon.

Wilderness Lodge

Artist Point
DDP: Two credits (T) / Cost: $$$ (TiW)
TYPE: Pacific Northwest/American; Fine/Signature; Dinner

If you have ever visited the legendary Ahwahnee Hotel in Yosemite (recently renamed the Majestic Yosemite Hotel in a trademark dispute), you'll feel right at home here. The Craftsman-style fixtures and National Park vibe are similar. It's rustic luxury at its best. Reservations are easier to obtain than at some of the other fine/signature hotels, so you just might be able to get into this gorgeous restaurant if the mood strikes you, particularly if you're here during the off-season.

The artisanal cheeses and charcuterie are exceptional. The wide variety of both will knock your socks off—very impressive! Other appetizers include shrimp cocktail, ahi tuna take, braised short rib bolognese with farm egg pappardelle, and steamed mussels. Smoked mushroom bisque, heirloom tomatoes, and greens salads are available. Steak, chicken, pork, bison, seafood including cedar-planked salmon, wild halibut "en Papillote," or oar-seared diver scallops are guaranteed to impress. Mickey Check meals are chicken or fish, but a petite steak and pasta are added on the children's menu. If you really want to embrace the best of the Northwest, try the five-course Taste of the Pacific *prix fixe* meal. It starts with a champagne toast and ends with some of the most decadent desserts this side of the Rocky Mountains. The absolutely beautiful chocolate crémeaux, a dressed-up vanilla bean crème brûlée, housemade warm donuts with dipping sauces, and other decadent choices will seal the deal. Specialty cocktails include the North Flight Martini, Raspberry Rapids, Lodge Fizz, and a Grand Margarita. The wine list here is an award-winning representation of the Pacific Northwest.

With all it has to offer, Artist Point just might become your new favorite Disney World dining place!

Whispering Canyon Café

DDP: One credit (T) / Cost: $-$$ (TiW)
TYPE: American; Unique/Themed; Breakfast, Lunch, and Dinner

Think rootin' and tootin' if you're planning to eat at the ironically named *Whispering* Canyon; this café is definitely *not* highfalutin.' It's buffet/family-style, with plenty of "antics" from the wait staff and lots going on to keep the kids occupied—Lincoln logs, coloring, sing-alongs, and hobby-horse races.

At breakfast, starters are fresh fruit with yogurt and granola, a heavenly sticky-bun skillet, and a blueberry muffin. Practically any American breakfast favorite you might crave is available, from a hearty skillet, eggs Benedict, egg-white omelette, ham-and-cheese omelette, chocolate chip or buttermilk pancakes, Belgian waffle, steel-cut oatmeal, and banana bread French toast. Lots of sides such as sausage, toast, grits, and biscuits and gravy will fill up the whole posse. Order French press coffee, juices, and many non-alcoholic beverages, plus they'll be happy to whip up a Bloody Mary or mimosa for you.

Lunch offers some appetizers you won't find everywhere, like pulled pork spring roll, chilled yellow tomato soup, incredible Indian fry bread with dipping sauces, Gold Rush western chips and queso, or a really snappy organic mixed greens salad (think Humboldt fog goat cheese, citrus vinaigrette, and pumpkin seed brittle). The all-you-care-to-enjoy skillet is a cowboy's dream—ribs, pulled pork, chicken, sausage,

Yukon potatoes, corn on the cob, and baked beans. Sandwiches are plentiful: bison burger, tuna melt, salmon BLT, chicken, turkey, pulled pork, and more. Could you still be hungry? Upscale western fare like Whispering Canyon pioneer chocolate cake or a Mason-jar cheesecake might tempt you. How about the Cowboy Hat Challenge? While it no longer appears on the standard menu and you'll pay handsomely for it, you could always make "puppy dog eyes" and ask for it nicely: Take a ten-gallon "hat" (don't worry, it's plastic) and fill with scoops of ice cream (chocolate, vanilla, strawberry, mint-chip) and smother it in "every topping from the chuck wagon." Throw in a couple of brownies, cookies, a slice of apple pie, and top with toasted marshmallows on a skewer. It serves four.

Dinner is every bit as down-home. Appetizers are the same as at lunch. Entrées are meatloaf, rainbow trout, NY strip steak, ribs, chili-crusted pork loin rib chop, skillet-fired red quinoa cakes, or one of those wowza cowboy skillets with everything a hard-workin' cowpoke desires. Desserts are the same as at lunch. Mickey Check meals are chicken, fish, or grilled cheese dippers. Red and white wines of the Pacific Northwest, draft and bottled beers, imaginative drinks like a Moonshine Flight and Magical Star Cocktail, and a happy assortment of non-alcoholic beverages including that amazing French press coffee will accompany your meal to perfection.

Pull yourself up a chair (Cowboys or Native Americans stenciled on the back), loosen your belt, and dig in. I guarantee you won't leave here hungry, partners!

Yacht Club Resort

Yachtsman Steakhouse
DDP: Two credits (T) / Cost: $$$
TYPE: American/Steakhouse; Fine/Signature; Dinner

Travel to New England without ever leaving Orlando. Some guests find the décor a bit plain, but the clean lines, knotty pine rafters, and maritime touches are appreciated by most. Although nautical, the entrée emphasis here is on steak.

Start your dinner with jumbo shrimp, calamari, cheeses, or the vast selection of charcuterie. A true carnivore's delight, you'll find 100% Japanese Wagyu beef, signature 21-day dry-aged steaks, and butcher's cuts on the menu *and* in a display window in case you'd like to select your own. Something different? Try the elk tenderloin, sea bass, braised beef short rib with polenta cream, lobster, chicken, or Okinawan sweet potato-filled pasta. Sides are truffle mac and cheese, creamed spinach, sautéed mushrooms, twice-baked potatoes, sautéed vegetable fricassee, a stunning spring pea risotto with bacon and pearl onions, or caramelized onions—yum. If your sweet tooth remains unsatisfied, you must give the chocolate-peanut cake a try—truly scrumptious. There's also lemon blueberry cheesecake, a sorbet trio, sugarless carrot cake, lime semifreddo with meringue and guava, crème brûlée, or the good old Yankee Yachtsman sundae. Mickey Check meals are grilled chicken or baked fish. Children's menu items also include mac and cheese, pasta and meatballs, or a steak skewer. Kids are sure to love the Mickey puzzle dessert (it's incredible) and the Toy Story 3 or Fairies punch. Four good Napa wines are joined by De Toren Z red blend from South Africa.

Thurston Howell the Third would feel right at home at the Yachtsman! So will you.

There you have it, the best of the best. Don't come looking for bargains here. You'll pay quite a premium for a wonderful meal at any of these fine/signature or unique/themed restaurants, but if you're looking for something out of the ordinary, a dining experience that will be remembered long after your vacation is over, then select a favorite from among these stellar places, make an advance dining reservation, sit back, and enjoy!

Dinner Shows and Character Meals

The Best of the Disney Resort Hotels

Menu items change frequently at Disney's dinner shows and character meals, and the characters themselves always appear *subject to availability*. This chapter will give you a reasonable idea of the general kinds of foods and experiences to expect, but *nothing* is guaranteed. Even two of the three dinner shows are subject to weather issues and can be cancelled at the last minute.

Beach Club Resort and Villas

Cape May Café
DDP: One credit (T) / Cost: $$ (TiW)
TYPE: American; Character Buffet; Breakfast
CHARACTERS: Donald, Goofy, Minnie—in beach attire

Dining at this attractive, quaint café will take you back to the turn of the twentieth century on the Atlantic seaboard. It's relaxing and a very simple way to be sure your party has a great opportunity to visit some of Disney's most popular characters. Meanwhile, you can all enjoy a bountiful all-you-care-to-enjoy breakfast buffet before beginning your day's activities.

Cold offerings might include salami, capicola (Corsican pork cold cut), sliced meats and cheeses, hard boiled eggs, low-fat cottage cheese, apple slices, fresh fruit, spinach salad, yogurt with house-made granola, bagels, assorted breads, and cold cereals. Hot offerings are items such as scrambled eggs, frittatas, ham, sausages, eggs with cheese and chorizo, bacon, cheddar grits, hot quinoa cereal, and biscuits with sausage gravy. In addition, you'll find many assorted freshly baked pastries.

It's such fun to get a chance to visit with the Disney characters while enjoying a delicious breakfast buffet. Prices are reasonable, and you won't leave hungry.

Contemporary Resort

Chef Mickey's Fun Time Buffet
DDP: One credit (T) / Cost: $$$ (TiW)
TYPE: American; Character Buffet; Breakfast, Brunch, and Dinner
CHARACTERS: Donald, Goofy, Mickey, Minnie, Pluto

Chef Mickey's is one of the most difficult dining reservations to obtain. It's always popular and competition for a table is intense. If you hope to dine here, you must start trying as early as you possibly can. The characters will lead guests in songs and dances as the monorails speed by.

Breakfast has a first plate course: smoked salmon, hard-boiled eggs, seasonal melons and other fruits, yogurt and granola, and quinoa salad. The second plate course is potato casserole, pancakes, ham, tofu/spinach scramble, and bacon or sausage. For the young Mouseketeers, there's a special buffet with scrambled eggs, tater tots, sausages, and Mickey waffles. Sweets include Krispy Kreme donut holes, cheese blitzes with toppings, danishes, and Minnie's muffins.

The brunch menu is more extensive, with heartier choices. To the first plate, peel-and-eat shrimp and seasonal salad selections are added. To the second plate, barbecue pork ribs and baked salmon join the menu, along with corned beef hash and vegetables. The Mouseketeers get chicken nuggets and mac and cheese. For the sweets and treats, those change to a build-your-own sundae bar, a Mickey Mousse dome (it's amazing!), assorted pastries, and chocolate chip cookies.

At dinner, the first plate is fresh mixed fruit salad, peel-and-eat shrimp, and salads. The second plate is pork ribs, chicken, salmon, mussels in tomato/fennel broth, and carving stations. The children will find a buffet stocked with nuggets, sloppy Joes, and mac and cheese. Sweets and treats are key lime and seasonal fruit tarts, the build-your-own sundae bar, and chocolate chip cookies. Four non-alcoholic specialty drinks and about twenty classic cocktails (Moscow Mule, Mt. Kilamarita Bahama Mama, Ultimate Long Island Iced Tea, Pimm's Punch, and Rye Manhattan, to name just a few) are available at dinner, along with the usual variety of non-alcoholic beverages.

The place will be packed, noisy, and it sometimes feels a bit chaotic. Some guests have complained of chicken nuggets ground into the carpet and roving bands of excited children trailing in Mickey's wake. Don't expect to savor a relaxing, quiet dinner here. It's worth asking to be seated in the main dining room where the action seems to be centered (since it's the characters you came to see, after all). Chef Mickey's is lively and exciting, but it's always *very* difficult to get a table.

Fort Wilderness Resort

Hoop-De-Doo Musical Revue Dinner Show

DDP: Two credits (T) / Cost: $$$-$$$$ (TiW, 9:30 p.m. show only)
TYPE: Country/American; Dinner Show; Dinner

There is a reason for the enduring popularity of the three Disney dinner shows (this one, Mickey's Backyard BBQ, and the Polynesian's Spirit of Aloha)—they are outstanding. Hoop-De-Doo celebrated its forty-year anniversary during the summer of 2014. By then, more than ten-and-a-half *million* guests had Hoop-De-Doo'ed, and with two or three shows a night, that was more than 37,000 performances.

Most shows are sold out. Check the seating chart at disneyworld.disney.go.com. Section three is upstairs, and there is no elevator. The chairs swivel for ease of service. You get a good view of the entire restaurant and stage. Section two is on the sides and in the back of the first floor. Section one is front and center. The difference in price between section one and section three is about $8 per adult. No need to scramble for a seat, as they are all reserved. There is a lot of audience participation—stompin' and hollerin' and the enthusiastic waving of napkins. You must prepay at the time you make reservations.

The show's location at Pioneer Hall is not accessible by car. You must allow *plenty* of time to get here. It isn't easy! From the

Magic Kingdom, you can catch a boat to Fort Wilderness. (If you take the bus, tack on at least fifteen or twenty extra minutes because you'll need to switch to a shuttle bus to reach Pioneer Hall.) There are songs, family-friendly jokes, corny vaude-ville-type routines, and all of it delivered with a country flavor.

Speaking of country, the meal is an all-you-care-to enjoy feast of fried chicken and barbecue pork ribs, tossed green salad, baked beans, cornbread, and strawberry shortcake, but with advance notice, special dietary requests can usually be accommodated.

The vast majority of guests love the whole experience. It is highly recommended, but you may have trouble getting a reservation, so book as early as you can.

Mickey's Backyard BBQ Dinner Show

DDP: Two credits (T) / Cost: $$-$$$ (TiW, 9:30 p.m. show only)
TYPE: Country/American; Dinner Show; Dinner
CHARACTERS: Chip, Dale, Mickey, Minne—dressed Western style

Entertainment includes a live country-western band, rope tricks, and audience participation line dancing. Several times throughout the evening, costumed characters come into the audience to visit with guests. The dining area is covered, but there is no protection from the elements on the open sides. You prepay for your tickets. If it is considered too cold or too rainy for comfort, the show can be cancelled at the last minute. Food includes hamburgers, hot dogs, smoked chicken, mac and cheese, barbecue ribs, and many side dishes. Cobbler and ice cream bars are served for dessert. To wash it down, there's lemonade and punch for the kids, beer and sangria for adults. You'll be eating at picnic tables, and the atmosphere is *very* casual. Plates, cutlery, and cups are plastic.

The show is held at the Fort Wilderness Pavilion, which is not easy to reach. From the Magic Kingdom, there's a boat directly to Fort Wilderness. By bus, you'll need to board a sepa-rate shuttle to get here. As with the Hoop-Dee-Doo Revue, allow *plenty* of time to arrive. If you book Category 1 seating, you get early access to the pavilion, but you must arrive at least one hour before the show. You also get the chance to meet and greet the characters before the rest of the diners, get first crack at the serve-yourself buffet, and are seated closer to the show.

The food is nothing special; it's just typical backyard barbecue fare (but the food isn't why people come). Children (of all ages) adore the show and practically everyone leaves in a good mood. You may be paying close to $60 for a hot dog, a Coke, and an ice cream bar, but as with most things Disney, the entertainment is very well done. All three dinner shows are incredibly popular.

Grand Floridian Resort and Spa

My Disney Girl's Perfectly Princess Tea Party

DDP: No / Cost: !!!! (see review)
TYPE: British/American; English-style Tea
CHARACTERS: Aurora and Rose Petal

Held in the Grand Floridian's Garden View Tea Room, this is one of the most expensive "experiences" you can provide for your little prince or princess at Walt Disney World. (Virtually every child will come in costume, many directly from the satellite branch of the Bibbidi Bobbidi Boutique in the Grand Floridian itself.) Say Mom and Dad want to treat their two daughters, ages 3–9, to tea with Aurora and Rose Petal. The cost for this family of four pretty quickly reaches $666, not including tax, for a couple of teensy, weensy pre-made sandwiches, a pot of tea for the adults (there *may* be a charge for extra pots of tea; check first to be sure), and a small one of apple juice for the kids, and another couple of little nibbles like a sesame cracker and grapes. (This makes Cinderella's Royal Table at $232 for the same family to have a luxurious, full-service, multi-course dinner look like a terrific bargain—and at least there, you meet *many* princesses and get an actual meal, not a skimpy snack.)

Now, to be fair, your children do get "gifts" at the tea party, gifts that you've pre-paid for handsomely. Girls receive an 18" Princess Aurora doll with accessories, a tiara, princess bracelet, princess necklace, a fresh rose, a sticker page "Best Friend" certificate for the Aurora doll, and a princess drawstring bag. Boys receive a sword and shield, souvenir pin, Disney stuffed bear, and "Best Friend" certificate.

How much exactly are we talking about? All this comes at a high price. The cost for one child (ages 3–9) and one adult is

$333.64 (there's a charge for "one adult" because you can't just drop off your kid; at least one adult is required to attend the tea party with their child). For additional children, it's $234.08 apiece, and for additional adults it's $98.66 apiece. If the adults in the party want to receive the same gifts that the children receive, you'll have to fork over an additional $136.22.

Some guests rate this tea party as an outstanding value, something their children remember fondly. Others are disappointed, even horrified, at what they received for the cost. You'll have to decide if meeting Aurora (not one of the most well-known or beloved of the royals) and Rose Petal ("a magical rose from Aurora's garden" who has come to life), having a few snacks (do your kids even *like* itty-bitty chicken curry or egg salad sandwiches?), and some "gifts" are worth such serious money.

In addition to the tea and snacks, there are sing-alongs, a princess parade, and storytelling by Rose Petal who acts as the hostess for the event. It's strictly your call, and your child(ren) might just *love* it, but by any reckoning, this tea party is one extremely expensive little cup of apple juice.

Wonderland Tea Party

DDP: No / Cost: $40 per child (ages 4-12), plus tax
TYPE: American; Character Tea Party
CHARACTERS: Alice and the Mad Hatter

This is a charming little hour-long tea party is for children between ages 4–12. They will have tea, aka apple juice, decorate a cupcake with sprinkles, made a craft, and have their photos taken with Alice and the Mad Hatter. Since it lasts about an hour and adults *aren't* included in the festivities, you might take the opportunity to have lunch or tea yourself and simply check out the beautiful grounds and exclusive, upscale shops of the Grand Floridian during that time. Some guests are concerned that the Mad Hatter might frighten their kids. If you're one of them, you might schedule the tea party toward the end of your vacation so that children are more used to the idea of costumed characters. At $40, this is a good value and one that comes highly recommended.

1900 Park Fare

DDP: One credit (T) / Cost: $$ (TiW)
TYPE: American; Character Buffet; Breakfast and Dinner
CHARACTERS (breakfast):
Mary Poppins, Winnie the Pooh, Tigger, Alice, Mad Hatter
CHARACTERS (dinner):
Cinderella, the Prince, Lady Tremaine, Anastasia, and Drizella

If you weren't able to secure a table at Cinderella Castle for breakfast, here's another opportunity for you to enjoy a character meal, and one that's *much* easier to book. No one trains its costumed characters like Disney. This "veddy Brrritish" crew of characters will cheerfully pose for pictures, sign autographs, and interact with guests at every one of the tables. Meanwhile, you and your group will be able to sit down to a delectable buffet breakfast before heading off to the parks. The all-you-care-to-enjoy buffet will satisfy most guests. All the non-alcoholic, non-specialty beverages are included in the price. There is a yogurt station with all the trimmings as well as a bagel station with assorted cream cheese spreads. Find plenty of scrambled eggs, bacon, sausage, pancakes, Mickey waffles, French toast, cheese blintzes, hash brown casserole, smoked salmon, and classic eggs Benedict. Oatmeal and assorted cold cereals are available, too. Look for the delicious chilled strawberry soup (seasonal) and fresh fruit. This is a relatively low-key, reasonably priced way to have a wonderful meal while interacting with those delightful Disney characters.

Dinner is your chance to meet the characters from *Cinderella* while your party sits down to a nice buffet dinner in a beautiful restaurant. It's far easier to book this reservation than Cinderella's Royal Table or Chef Mickey's. The price is reasonable for the all-you-care-to-enjoy meal. There are more than a dozen varieties of salads on display. Visit the carving station for beef strip loin and the stir-fry station. You'll find more to choose from than you could possibly imagine. Look for sushi rolls, pot stickers, Asian barbecue ribs, seafood boil, peel-and-eat shrimp, gumbo, red beans and rice, couscous, chicken, salmon, and the list goes on and on. Watermelon soup and fresh fruit salad are frequent features at the buffet. The children's buffet is loaded with kid-friendly fare like mac and cheese, chicken drumsticks, pasta, pizza, and sides. As usual, the buffet dessert offerings are plentiful, tasty, and intended to please most guests. You'll have the chance to interact and pose for pictures with the characters, and it is highly entertaining to see them behaving as they would in the fairy tale. The handsome prince might even bestow a kiss on your own little princess's hand.

Polynesian Village Resort

'Ohana

DDP: One credit (T) / Cost: $$-$$$ (TiW)
TYPE: Polynesian; Unique/Themed; Breakfast (Character) and Dinner
CHARACTERS (breakfast): Lilo, Stitch, Pluto, Mickey

The restaurant calls to mind a tropical paradise with lots of carved Tikis and sea creatures suspended overhead. Look for 'Ohana on the upper floor of the resort's main lobby. It's gorgeous and lots of fun for all ages.

The Best Friends Character Breakfast is all-you-care-to-enjoy. Service here is usually (but not always) attentive, and you won't often have to wait long for refills. Juice and coffee come for the table, followed by family-style platters of scrambled eggs, bacon and sausage, potatoes, and sweet pineapple/assorted breakfast breads, Mickey waffles, and fresh fruit. It would be pretty difficult to get it wrong, and most guests are very pleased with the 'Ohana breakfast. The characters come to every table to pose for pictures and sign autographs. The characters are friendly and accommodating. It's a delightful meal with plenty of good food and good times. Don't be late to your assigned time! You'll be sorry if you are. Who knows when you can next be seated? You want to get to the parks at a reasonably early time, not be stuck cooling your heels in the Polynesian lobby.

Dinner has no characters, which is too bad because they add such fun to breakfast. Reviews are mixed, as is usual for any restaurant, but there are far more happy diners than disgruntled ones. If you are unhappy with your server or some aspect of your meal, politely alert management right away. Don't let it spoil what ought to be a wonderful experience for your party. At dinner, delicious pineapple bread and salad come out first. Chicken wings and pork dumplings are the appetizers.

Skewers of chicken, steak, and shrimp roasted over a tremendously huge pit are next. The steak seems to be the source of some complaints. Advise your server *clearly* about your preferences for doneness. Noodles and veggies are accompaniments. Rave reviews are garnered for the dessert, which is warm bread pudding with bananas and caramel sauce. Save room!

Disney's Spirit of Aloha Dinner Show

DDP: Two credits (T) / Cost: $$$$ (TiW, late show only)
TYPE: Polynesian; Dinner Show; Dinner

Spirit of Aloha is performed in a covered, but open-air theatre. If it is considered too cold or too rainy for comfort, the show can be cancelled at the last minute. As with all of the dinner shows, you pay in advance for your meal. There are three categories of seating. Check online at waltdisneyworld.go.com to familiarize yourself with them. Category 3 is on the upper floor and also at the far left and right sides of the main floor. Category 2 is on the sides of the main floor and at the center of the upper floor. Category 1 is front and center of the main floor. The difference in price between an adult sitting in Category 3 vs. Category 1 is about $12. Some guests complain that posts can obscure the view, so be clear on your expectations when booking your reservations.

The lively show includes hula dancing, fire dancing, and dances from Tahiti, Hawaii, Samoa, Tonga, and New Zealand. Food is somewhat more upscale than at either of the other two dinner shows, but you are really paying for the show, not the food. Getting here is far easier than getting to Fort Wilderness. The Polynesian is accessible by car, bus, or monorail, and even on foot from the Transportation and Ticket Center.

Dinner includes a fresh, green salad with ginger-lime dressing, platters of pulled pork, beef ribs, roasted chicken, and a vegetable medley. Children can order entrées such as mini corn dogs and tater tots, cheese pizza, grilled fish, or grilled chicken with rice and green beans. Unlimited beverages include Coke products, coffee, lemonade, beer, and wine. There are also fruity, specialty cocktails served in souvenir carved coconuts—those cost extra. To end the dinner ends, there's coconut guava cake with chocolate crunch.

The show, like all the dinner shows, is highly enjoyable, especially for children, and you'll find many families in attendance. Guests enjoy the traditional dancing, but many rate the show's story plot as a little "corny." The Spirit of Aloha is an extremely popular show and the all-you-care-to-enjoy dinner is filling.

There you have it, Disney World's three dinner shows and resort hotel character meals. Every one of them has something special to recommend it. You just have to decide what's the best choice for you and your family. None of them are inexpensive, but some are far more costly than others. Regardless of your choices, you're sure to enjoy your vacation if you put some time and effort into planning.

Now that we've completed our dining tour of all four theme parks, the BoardWalk, Disney Springs, the best resort hotel restaurants, the dinner shows, and the hotel character meals, it's time for me to let you in on a few tricks. The last chapter is filled with tried-and-true tips for getting those very difficult to obtain advance dining reservations. Follow this advice and you'll vastly improve your chances for making magical vacation memories to last a lifetime. This is the way my family and I book our ADRs, and believe me, it works! We always get the ADRs we want, and you can, too!

Getting Hard-to-Get ADRs
Twelve Tremendous Tips

Tremendous Tip #1

When making ADRs on B-Day (Booking Day) every single minute counts! Once the available booking slots have all been filled, you're out of luck. Therefore, have *two* (or more) adult members in your party ready to go on *two* (or more) separate computers (or iPhones or iPads) at 5:45 a.m. *Orlando time* on the very first day you are allowed to make your advance dining reservations. You will each need separate login names and passwords, too. Become familiar with how the system works well *before* the B-Day actually arrives. Both of you should already have your Magic Your Way reservation number, your credit card data, and *all* relevant information already loaded and on file so that when the clock strikes 6:00 a.m., you can *both* begin working simultaneously on securing the dining reservations. You take half, and let your partner take the other half. You'll *double* your chances of success. (Three of you working together can *triple* it.) Practice makes perfect, so practice, practice, and practice some more before your special morning arrives. That's not the time to fumble around looking for information. Read this tip *again* before you are ready to make your ADRs.

Tremendous Tip #2

If you've booked a Magic Your Way package, you can actually make those ridiculously hard-to-get Advance Dining Reservations up to 190 days (instead of the usual 180 days) ahead of your trip, assuming you're staying in a Disney accommodation for ten days. Sometimes, you will see this "loophole" referred to as 180+10. If you're staying at the resort for seven days, then you can book dining reservations 187 days in advance, etc. That way, you can reserve Cinderella's Royal Table at the end of your trip and *get up to a ten-day jump* on the rest of the public who will be madly scrambling to secure a table 180 days ahead of their trip. It is well worth remembering this!

Tremendous Tip #3

Book as many Advance Dining Reservations as you think you might possibly need. You can always cancel 24 hours ahead of time, but trying to book something "hot" at the last minute is extremely difficult if not downright impossible. (Just be sure you don't forget to cancel the ones you don't plan to use 24 hours before they're due or you'll be charged $10 per person in your party.) As your mother always told you, it's better to have it and not need it than to need it and not have it!

Tremendous Tip #4

Checking online *and* by phone 24 hours ahead of when you want to dine at a hard-to-schedule restaurant just *might* get you in. Remember that $10 per person cancellation fee if you miss the 24-hour cancellation deadline? Guests whose plans have changed at the last minute or who've decided they no longer want a reservation they made months before will be cancelling their ADRs a day ahead of time to avoid paying that fee. Sometimes, getting the reservation another guest just released simply comes down to luck. Good luck!

Tremendous Tip #5

Guests who need to cancel their entire Walt Disney World package have up to forty-five days before arriving to do so without a financial penalty. You should try checking *45 days before you are due to arrive* to see if anything you wanted (but didn't get) in the way of dining reservations might have opened up.

Tremendous Tip #6

As a last resort, try to book an ADR on the *same* day you want to dine at a particular restaurant. This is definitely a hit-or-miss strategy, mostly miss, but every once in a while, you'll get lucky and score that table at the last minute because someone else's plans unavoidably changed and they weren't able to cancel 24 hours before. While you are standing in line waiting to board an attraction, that's the perfect time to repeatedly dial and redial the restaurant you hoped to visit if you were unable to secure a reservation there earlier. Tables do occasionally open up at the last minute, for a variety of reasons. As a *very* last resort, try walking up to the host/hostess on duty and asking very politely for a table. Smile! It really does help. If you don't get what you want, be nice to the cast member anyway.

Tremendous Tip #7

Prioritize your picks! The most difficult dining reservations to book are the character meals (Cinderella's Royal Table, Chef Mickey's, 'Ohana, the Crystal Palace, etc), the dinner shows (Mickey's Backyard BBQ, the Hoop-De-Doo Musical Revue, and the Spirit of Aloha), places to dine at Epcot with good views of IllumiNations such as the Rose and Crown or La Hacienda de San Angel, the ones at the Magic Kingdom with views of the Happily Ever After fireworks like the California Grill and Narcoossee's, hugely popular restaurants like Canada's Le Cellier Steakhouse, Flying Fish on the Boardwalk, Be Our Guest at the Magic Kingdom, and Victoria & Albert's at the Grand Floridian. Decide which dining experiences are most important for you and your family and rank them in order.

Tremendous Tip #8

Use the "Wish List" function (again, well *before* your Booking Day arrives) on My Disney Experience (the special area of of the Walt Disney World website where guests are able to view and manage their reservations and vacation packages) and add the *most important* restaurants where you want to dine to create your very own Wish List. Then, when you are ready to make your dining reservations 190 days ahead of time (or 189 if you are staying at the resort for nine days, 188 days if you are staying eight days, 187 if you're staying a week, etc.), that quick link will save you precious moments. Don't waste even a second trying to type in the restaurants/character meals/dinner shows you want during your golden window of opportunity. It will take too much time. That window snaps shut very quickly. Once it's closed, you will just have to try some of the other tips to get an ADR.

Tremendous Tip #9

Type in the most important dining reservation *before* 6:00 a.m. on the very first day you are allowed to book. If you and one or two other adults in the party are dividing up the critical reservations into smaller, more manageable chunks, so much the better. It will increase your chances of getting what you want. Key in your highest priority reservation at 5:45 a.m. and the website will say something like "you cannot make your reservation at this time," and while that's true, as soon as 6:00 a.m. rolls around, all *you* have to do is hit "submit." Suddenly, your chances of dining with Cinderella are looking a lot more rosy. (If you feel you can't work this online feature, you'll simply have to wait until 7:00 a.m. Orlando time to book by telephone at 1-800-WDW-DINE. By that time, faster fingers will have grabbed most—if not all—of the most coveted spots and times. It might be worth asking a techie friend, or maybe a friend's computer-savvy son or daughter, to walk you though the process so you'll feel confident and prepared.)

Tremendous Tip #10

Book breakfast as early as possible near the most popular attractions in the parks to avoid long waits. It can save you the use of a FastPass+. This doesn't work for every park, but if you can get a jump on the rest of the guests who will be still waiting for the gates to open, so much the better. Be ready to finish your meal rapidly and head for the queues as soon as you possibly can. For example, dine at Be Our Guest at 8:00 a.m. Then, eat and immediately afterward head to the Seven

Dwarfs Mine Train or Peter Pan—two of the busiest attrac-tions in the entire Magic Kingdom. Breakfast at Tusker House in the Animal Kingdom gets you out on a safari early. Break-fast at Akershus Royal Banquet hall in Epcot can secure your party a coveted place on a Frozen Forever After boat earlier than would otherwise be possible. Breakfast at Hollywood and Vine in the Hollywood Studies at 8:00 *might* save a long wait at Rock 'n' Roller Coaster or the Twilight Zone Tower of Terror *if* you can get in and out quickly, but it's not very close to either of them (they are over on Sunset Boulevard)—and sometimes the entrance rope drops earlier than advertised at Hollywood Studios, letting guests in ahead of the announced time. In addition, guests have complained that even *with* 8:00 a.m. reservations, they weren't seated until as late as 8:40 AM, which entirely defeats the purpose of getting there early.

Tremendous Tip #11

A somewhat less scrupulous but nonetheless effective tip? If you're a couple, a party of two, it's a lot harder to score in-demand reservations, since most Disney restaurants have far fewer "tables for two" than they do family-sized tables for four. Therefore, if you indicate on the reservation app that you're a party of two, you're at an immediate disadvantage. If, instead, you try to book a reservation for three, Disney will open up the family-sized queue and you'll stand a better chance of getting the reservation. The unscrupulous part? When you get to the restaurant, you have to tell them at check-in that the third person in your party couldn't make it. They'll still seat you at a table for four, unless a table for two has magically popped up in the meantime. While it's probably not the best way to start your meal, it just might work for you in a pinch—*especially* if you're desperate.

Tremendous Tip #12

Go *in person* to the concierge at a deluxe resort hotel and ask for a reservation if none are available online or by phone. Cancella-tions are often "corralled" in the system expressly for concierge use (not for more than a few hours) before they're released into the general queue. Needless to say, be as polite and grateful as possible. The concierge is doing you a substantial *favor*. Remember when Grandma said you'd catch more flies with honey than with vinegar? Your attitude and demeanor *do* matter. Again, if you don't get what you hoped for, be nice anyway.

One final thing to clearly understand about your ADRs: a table is *not* going to be held empty awaiting your arrival. This fact is the source of much disappointment and unhappiness on the part of guests. Your reservation *only* entitles you to the next available table. If people are slow to vacate, you'll be left cooling your heels. No, it's not the way most reservations work anywhere else in the country, but it's the way reservations work at Walt Disney World. There is no way around this policy, so bear it in mind. Yours should be the group that arrives several minutes *earlier* than your actual reservation time.

Bon appétit, buen provecho, gutten appetit, velbekomme, selamat makan, buon apetito, smaklig måltid. Enjoy your meal!

Acknowledgments

Thanks to my wonderful family for their love and support; my late husband, Ron, always held dear in our hearts and memories; daughter Liz and her husband Amos; their children Katherine and Drew; son Rob and his wife, Catherine, and their baby, William. We've enjoyed many happy meals together at Walt Disney World, at Disneyland, and on the Disney *Magic* cruise. We look forward to many more as the kids grow up and their tastes change from nuggets to filets, from Mickey ice-cream bars to crème brûlées.

Loyal, lovely friends Anne, Linda, and Meg have been such bright lights in my life since my family moved to Iowa three decades ago. Iowa is a special place, the heart of the heartland, and my relationship with them is a perfect example of how this state nurtures much more than just corn—it also grows meaningful, loving friendships.

Book Club friends Margaret, Wendy, Jane, Becky, Dell, and Sheral are smart, funny, and wise. I've read more widely, thought more carefully, and written more accurately because of their kind mentoring. They lead by example, and I'm proud to know each and every one. I look forward to sharing many more adventures in the pages of books with them.

Last, but very definitely not least, thanks to Bob McLain, editor, writing guide, and inexhaustible curator of all things Disney. There isn't much this erudite scholar doesn't know about the subject, and I'm touched and honored that he has edited five of my books. With the experts among his authors, I'm humbled to be counted in their number. Thank you for everything, Bob!

Index

About the Author

Andrea McGann Keech grew up in southern California. Andrea and husband Ron met at Occidental College and were married in San Francisco. Ron graduated from the University of California at San Francisco Medical School, and Andrea finished college at the University of San Francisco. They lived in Portland, Oregon, for six years and then moved to Iowa City where he was a professor of medicine and surgeon in the Department of Ophthalmology at the University of Iowa for twenty-two years until his death. Their children Elizabeth and Robert made them very proud and very happy parents. Liz is an attorney, and Rob is a dentist.

Andrea taught students in English and Spanish in grades K-12 during her teaching career. She was a member of the National Assessment of Educational Progress Committee that established Writing Standards, 2011–2018, for students in grades 3–12. She has written for a variety of national educational journals and presented often at teaching conferences, but the most gratifying aspect of her work, by far, was seeing her students succeed. Andrea lives in Iowa City with Shadow and Sunny, two wild and crazy standard poodles. Her most fulfilling role is that of playing Mary Poppins to beloved grandchildren Katherine and Drew and spending time with baby grandson William.

Her other Disney books include *The Cream of the Crop: Tour Guide Tales from Disneyland's Golden Years*, *The Indulgent Grandparent's Guide to Walt Disney World*, *Walt Disney World Characters 101: Your Guide to Perfect Meet-and-Greets*, and *Treasure of the Ten Tags: A Disneyland Adventure*, all published by Theme Park Press.

ABOUT THEME PARK PRESS

Theme Park Press publishes books primarily about the Disney company, its history, culture, films, animation, and theme parks, as well as theme parks in general.

Our authors include noted historians, animators, Imagineers, and experts in the theme park industry.

We also publish many books by first-time authors, with topics ranging from fiction to theme park guides.

And we're always looking for new talent. If you'd like to write for us, or if you're interested in the many other titles in our catalog, please visit:

www.ThemeParkPress.com

. . . .

Theme Park Press Newsletter

Subscribe to our free email newsletter and enjoy:

- ◆ Free book downloads and giveaways
- ◆ Access to excerpts from our many books
- ◆ Announcements of forthcoming releases
- ◆ Exclusive additional content and chapters
- ◆ And more good stuff available nowhere else

To subscribe, visit www.ThemeParkPress.com, or send email to newsletter@themeparkpress.com.

Read more about these books
and our many other titles at:

www.ThemeParkPress.com

Made in the USA
San Bernardino, CA
14 December 2017